The Insect Coloring Book
By
Matthew E. Breer

An adult coloring book, Inspired by Illustrations of Bugs and creepy crawlies!

Over 40 illustrations for hours of stress relieving fun!

This book makes a perfect gift for everyone!

Be sure to check us out on Facebook and our website for other great things!

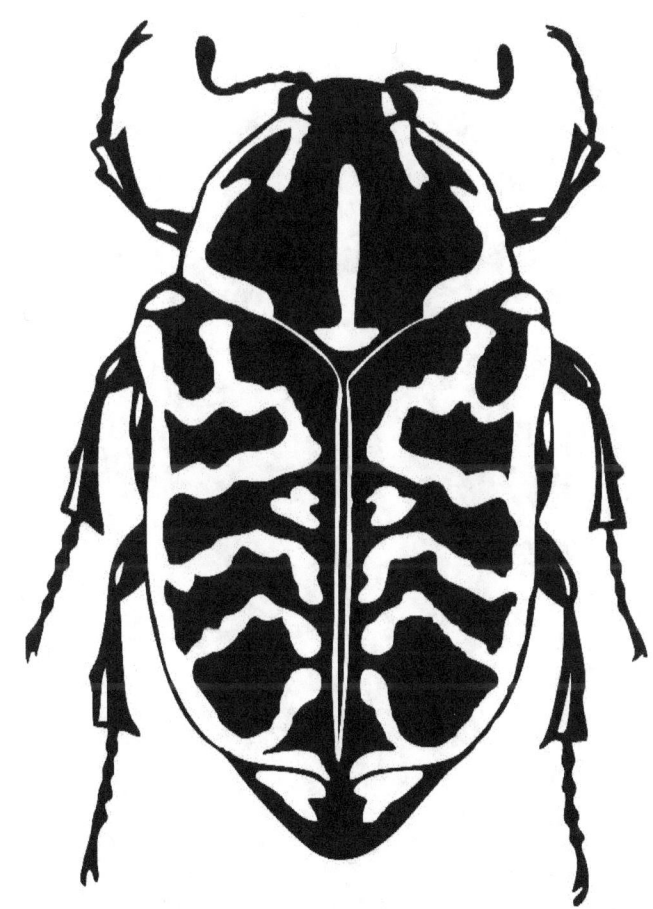

http://breerspublishing.weebly.com/

https://www.facebook.com/BreersPublishing/

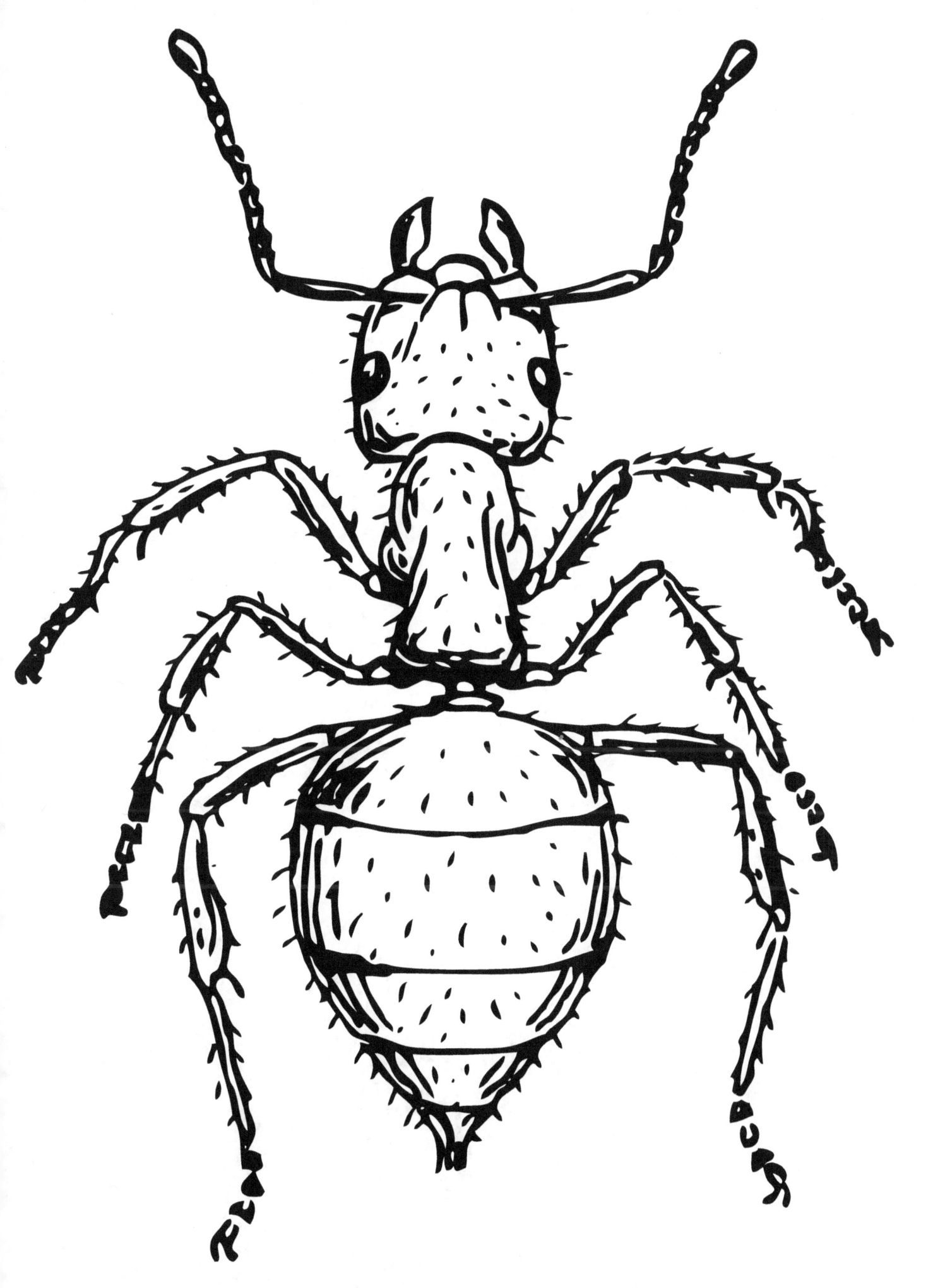

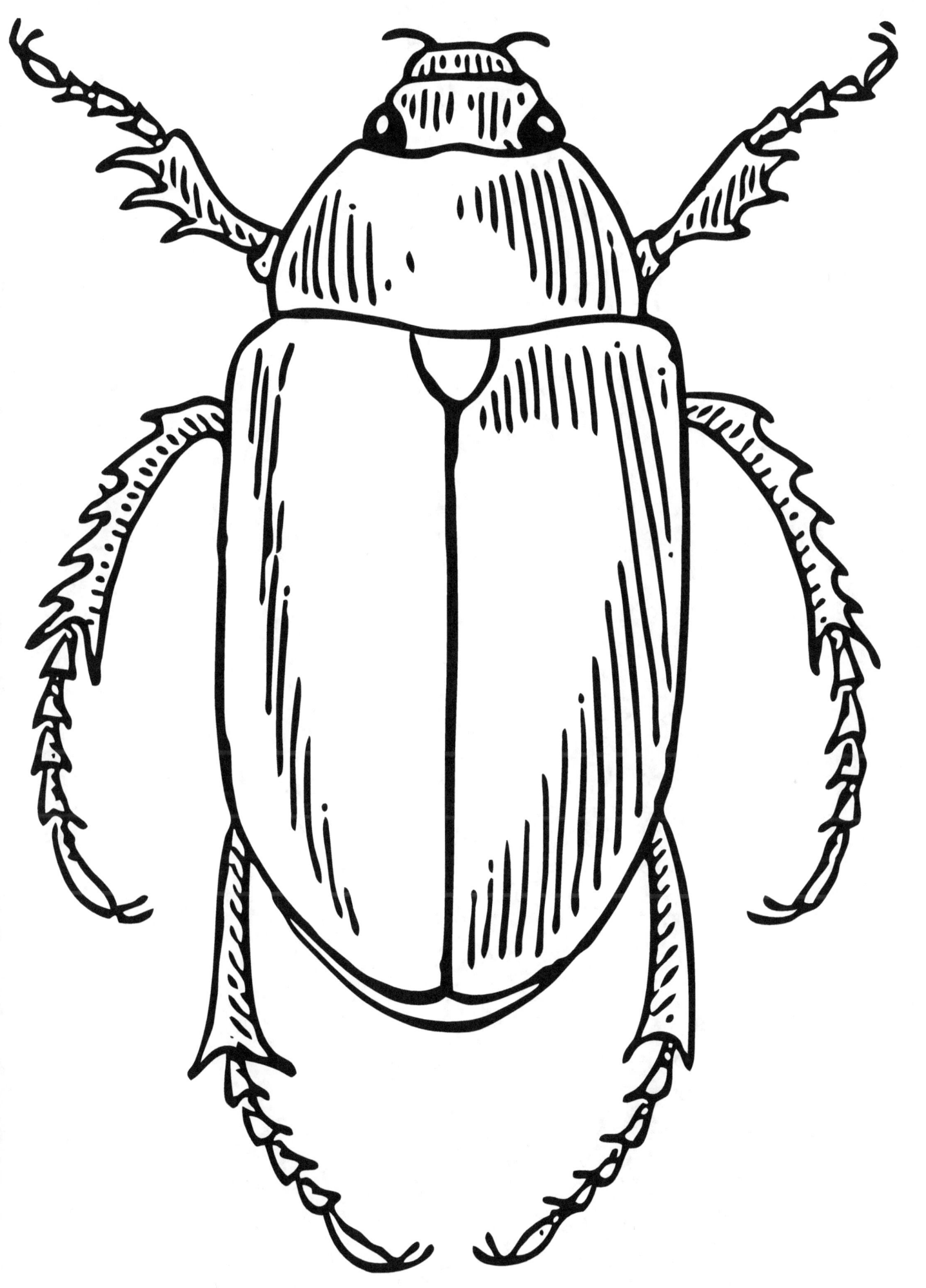

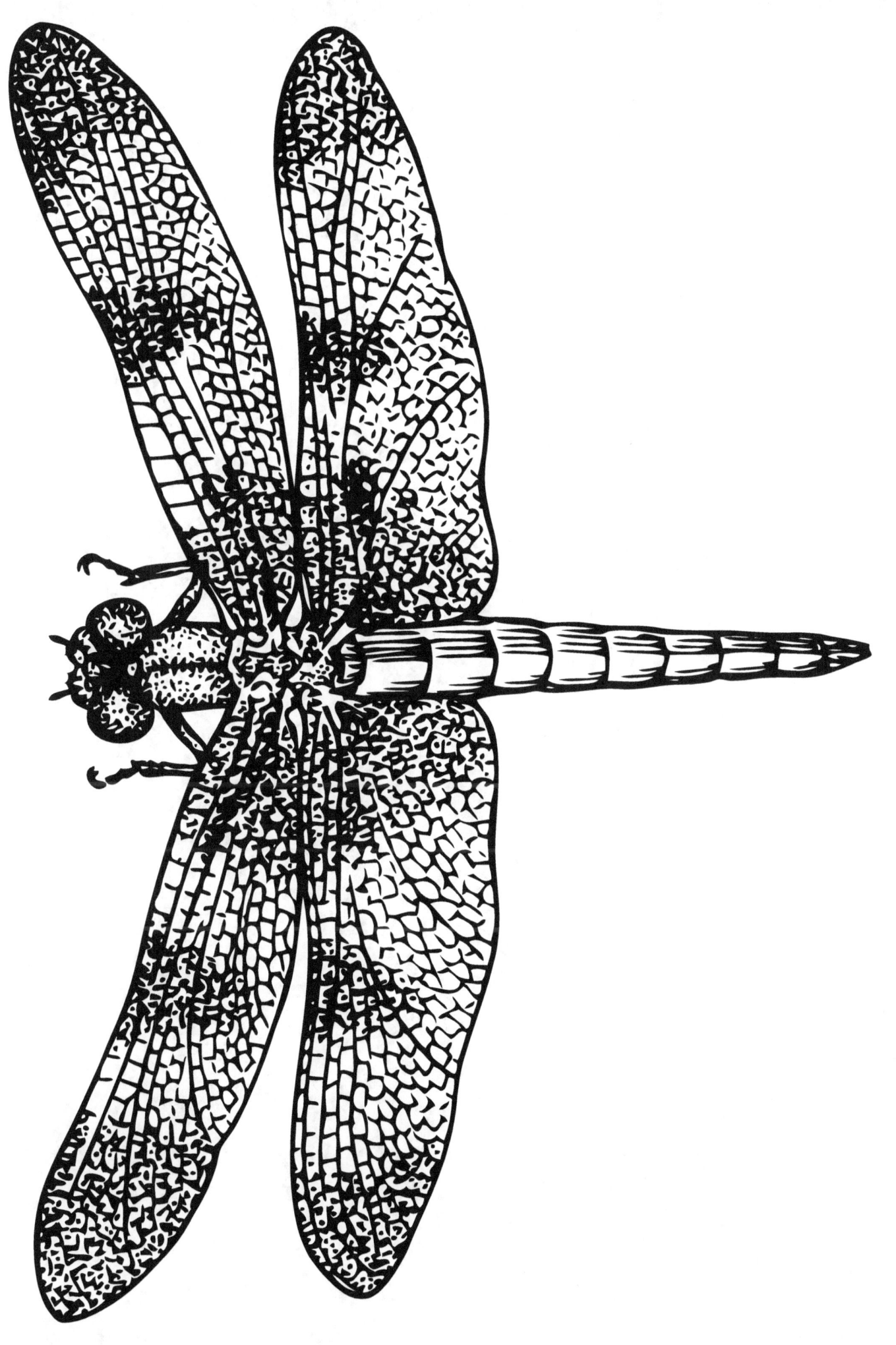

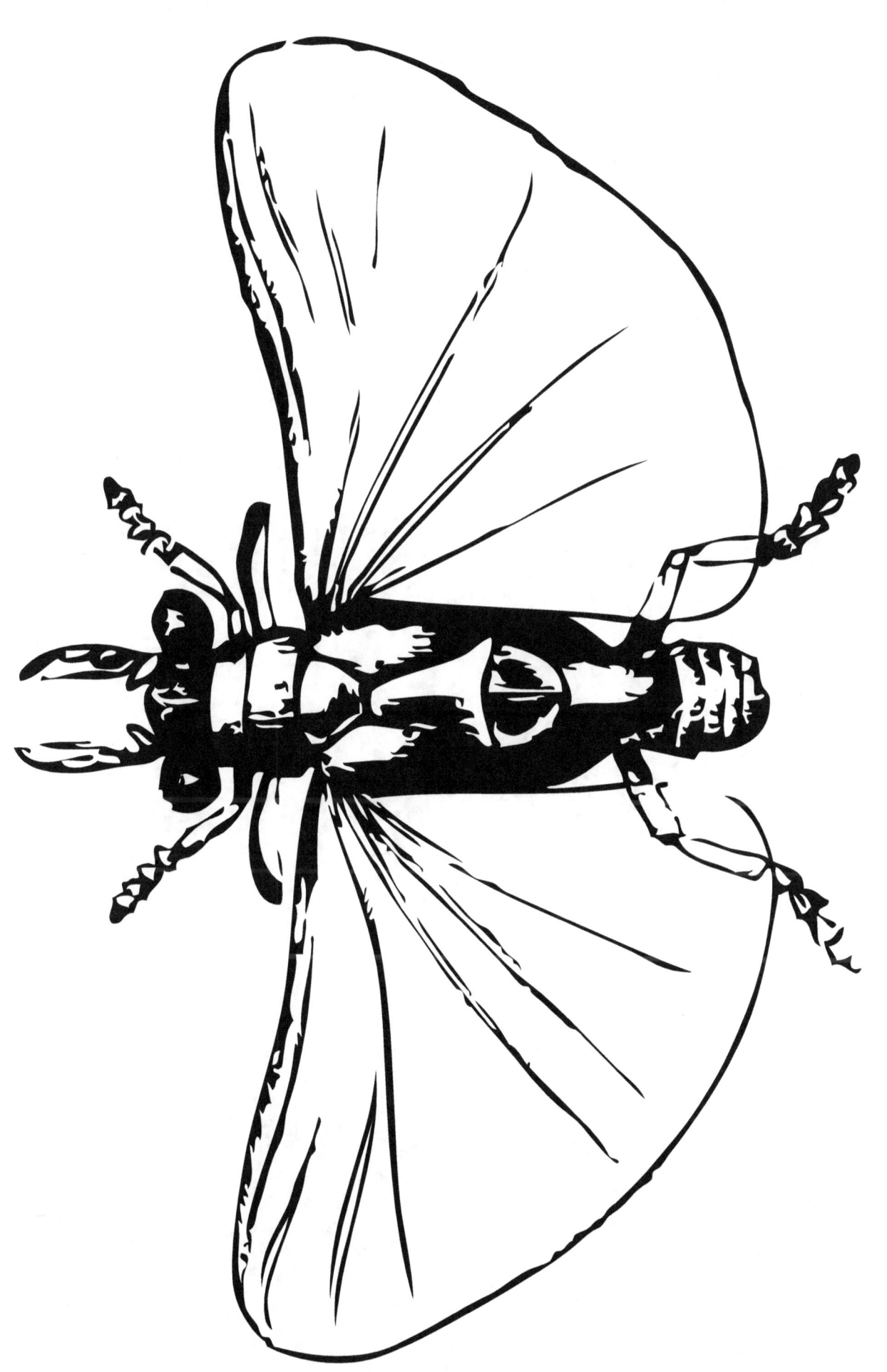

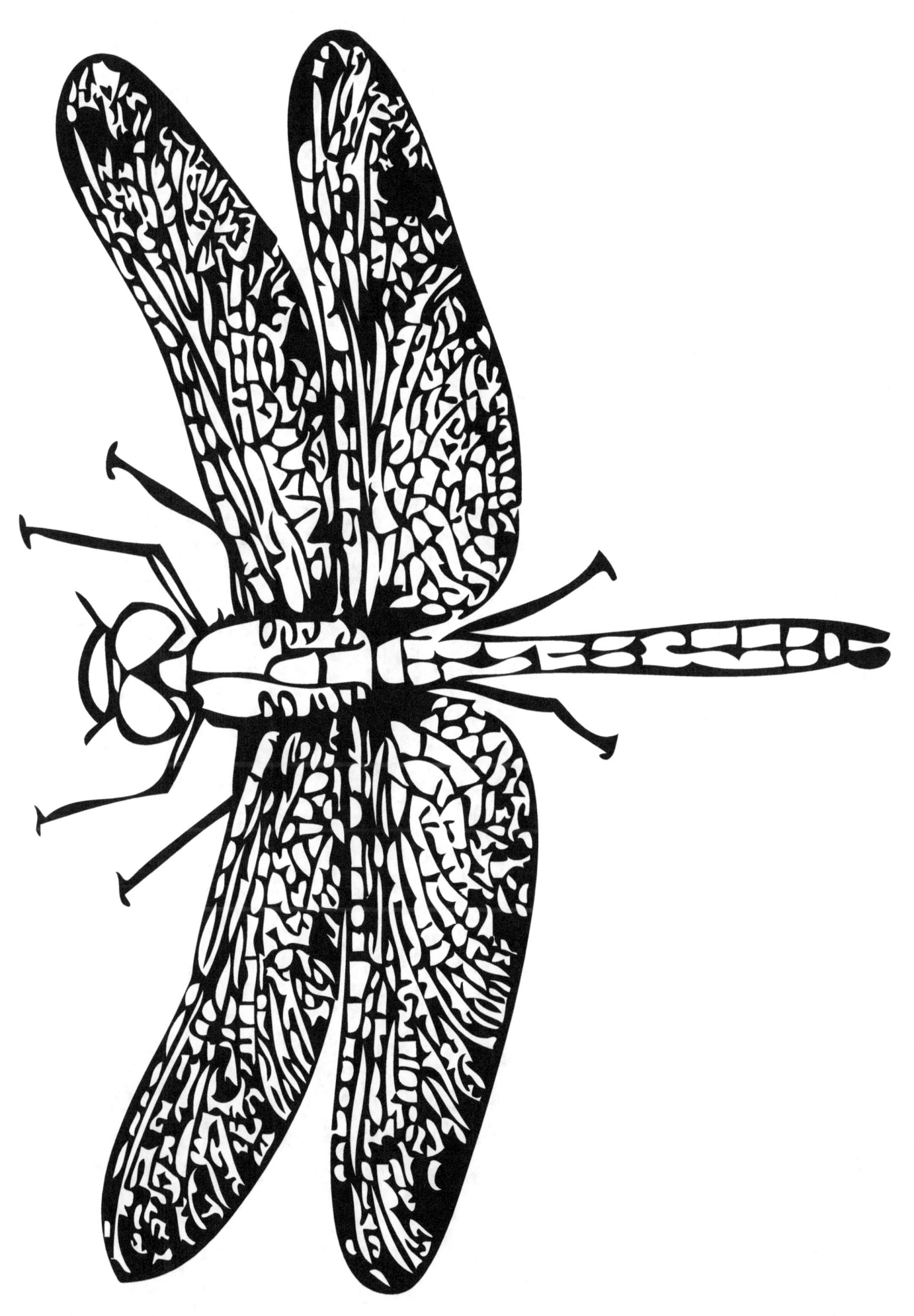

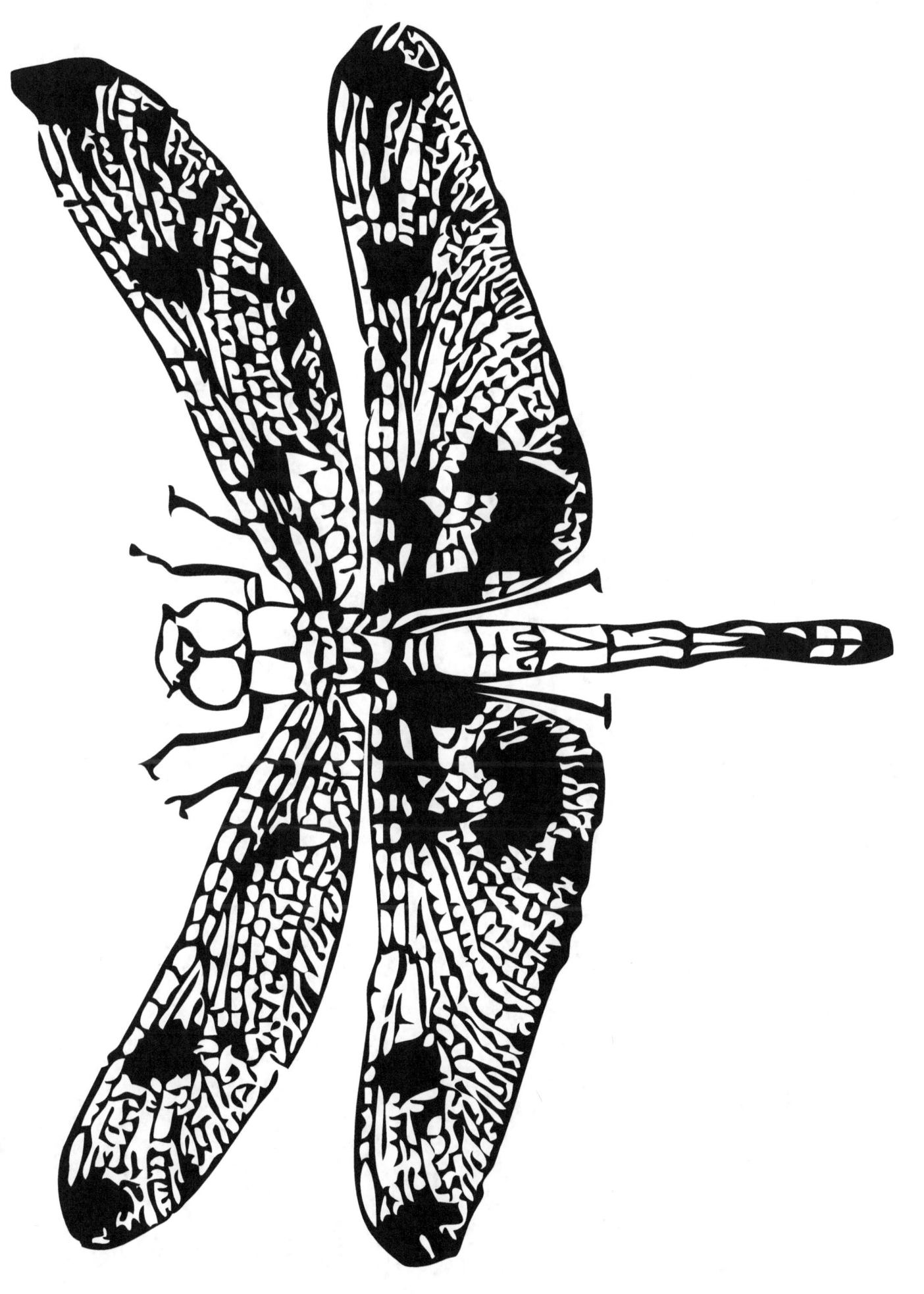

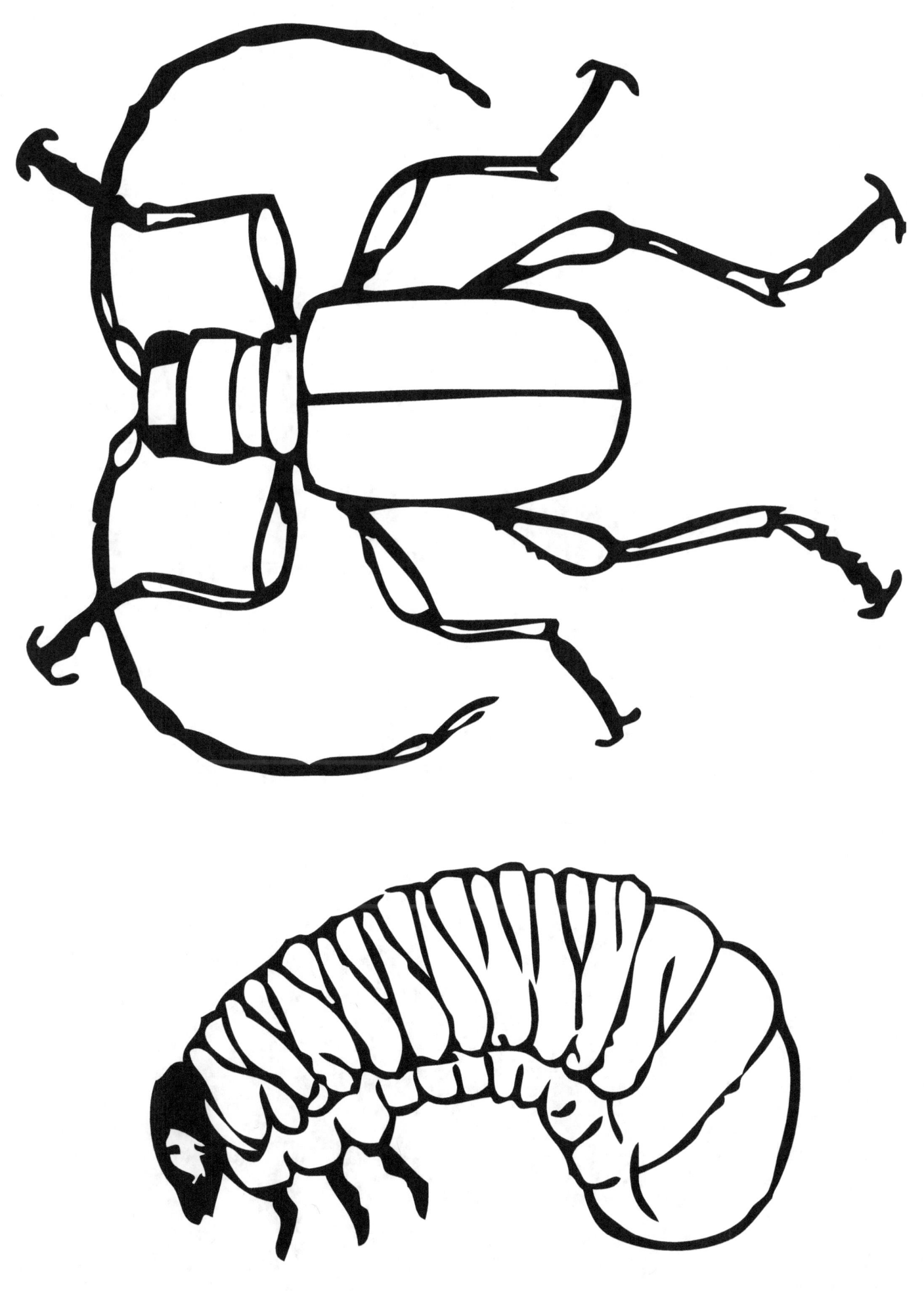

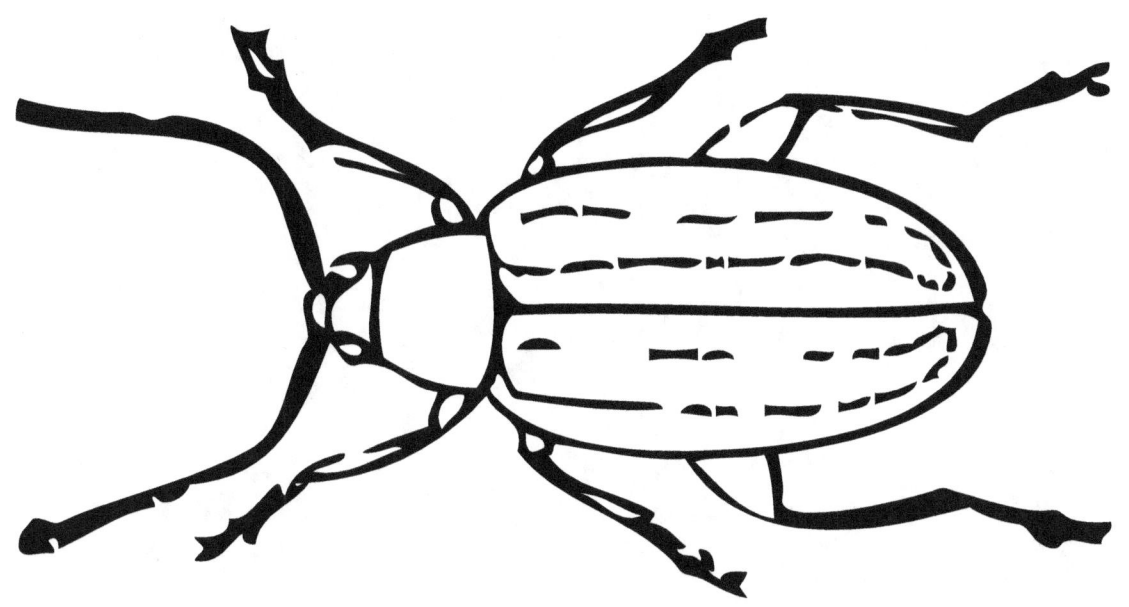

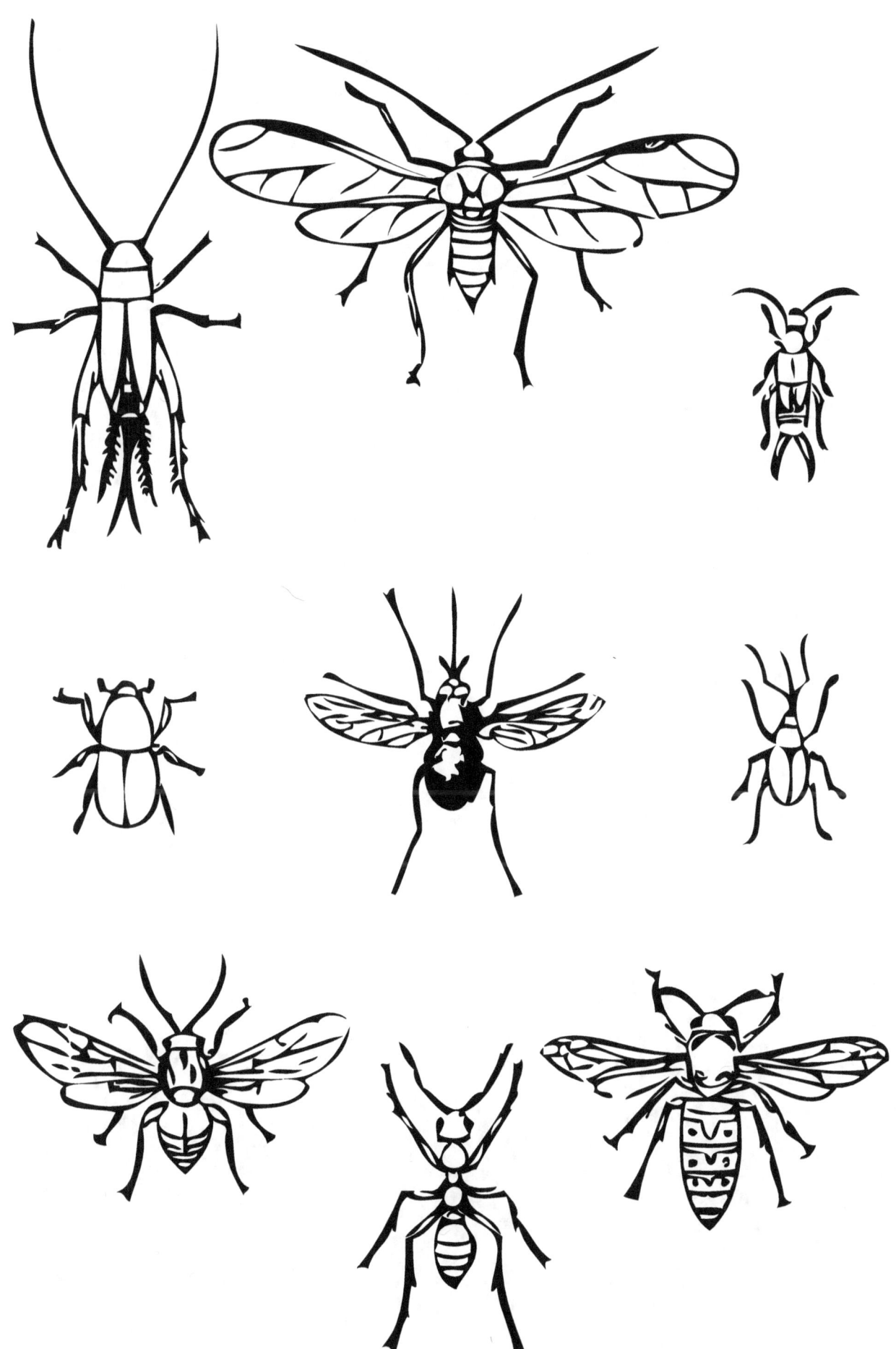

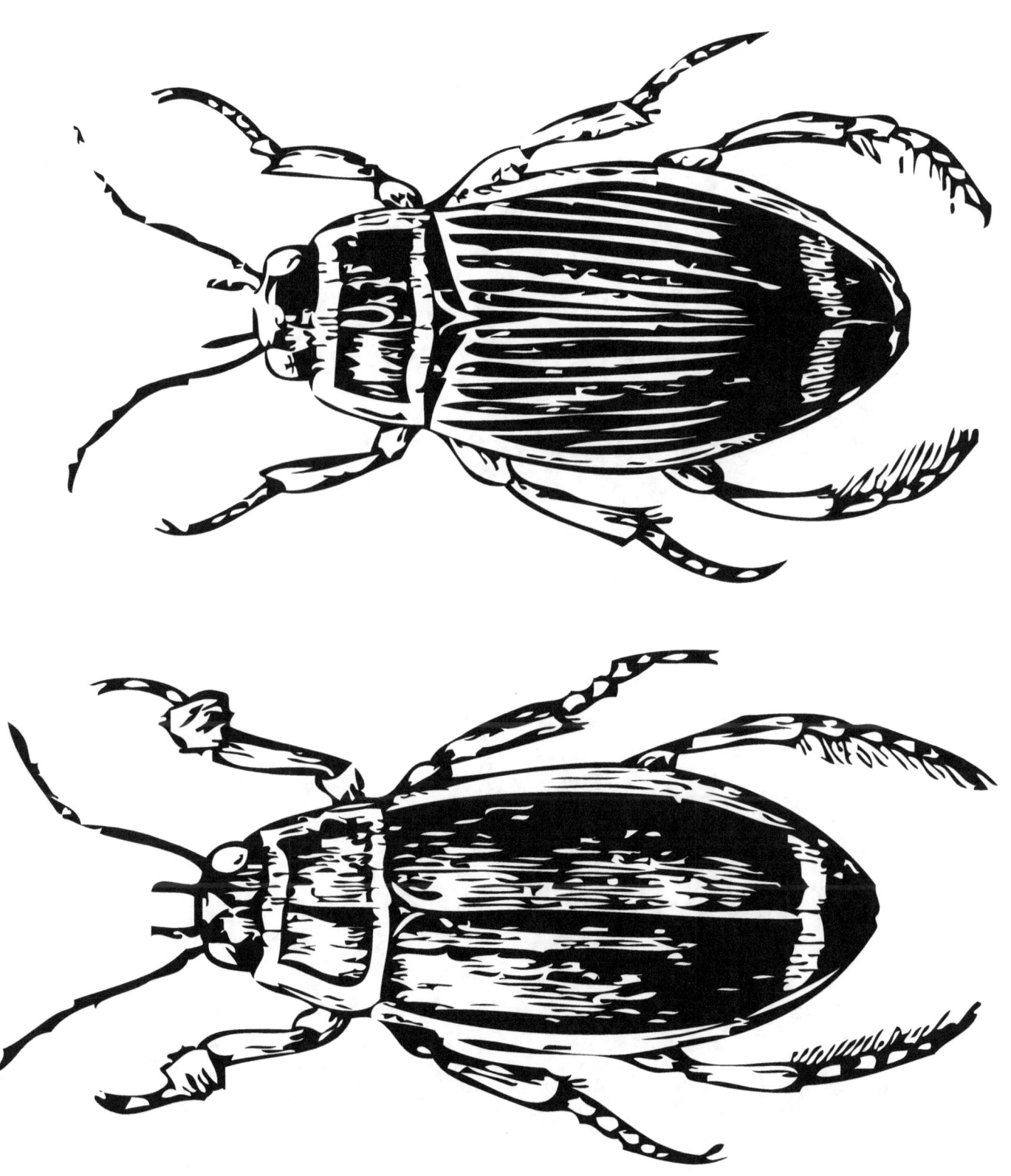

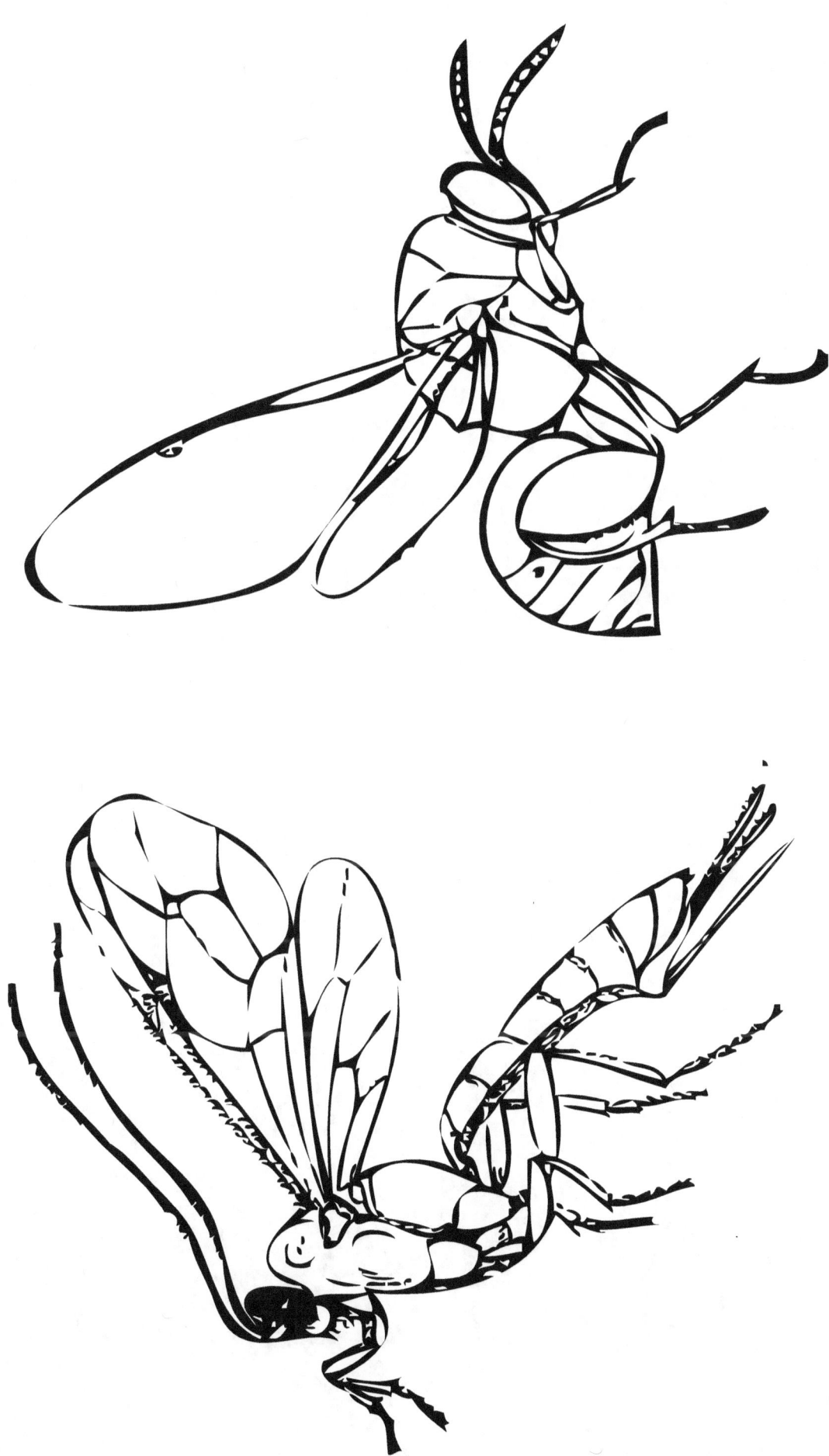

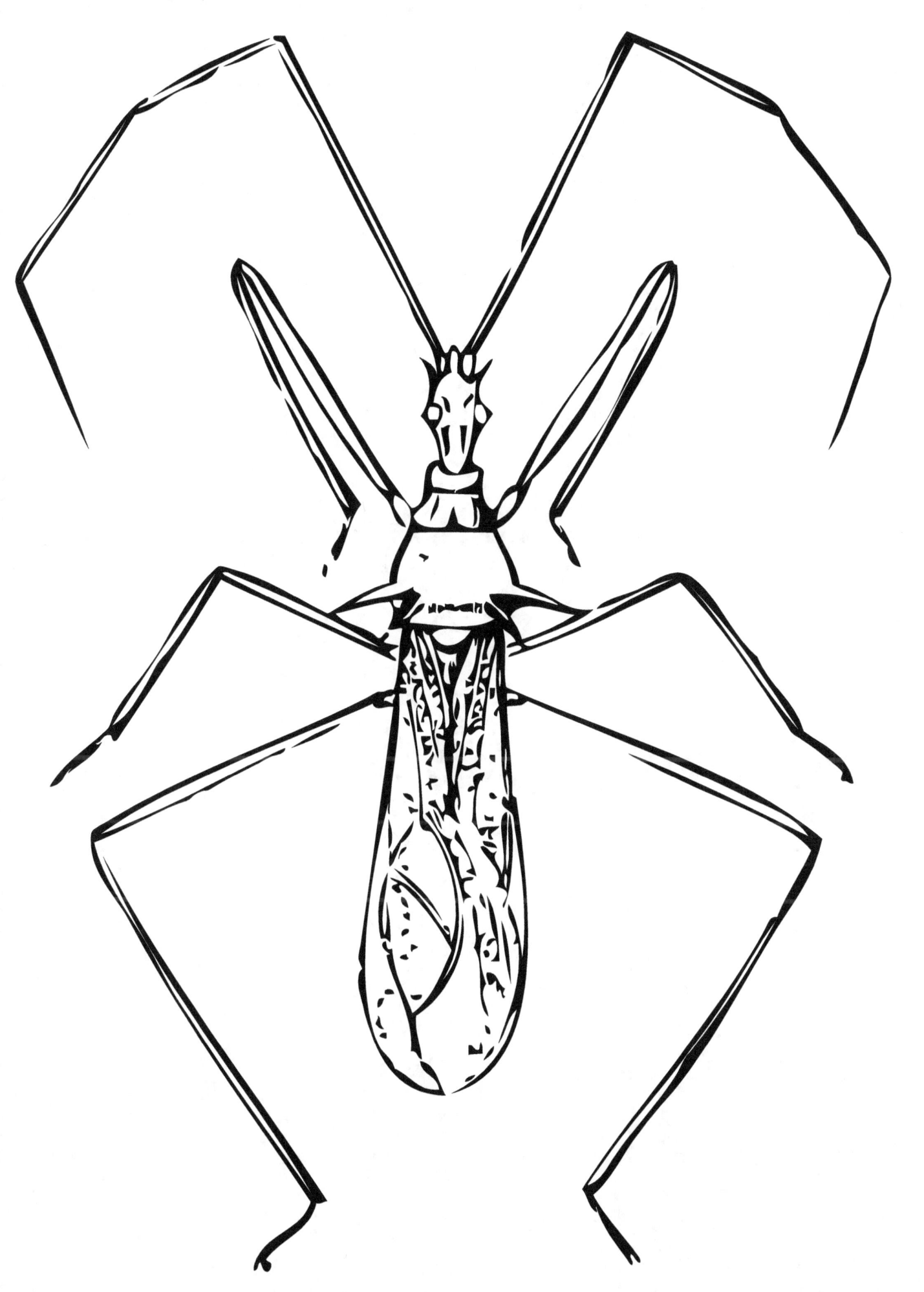

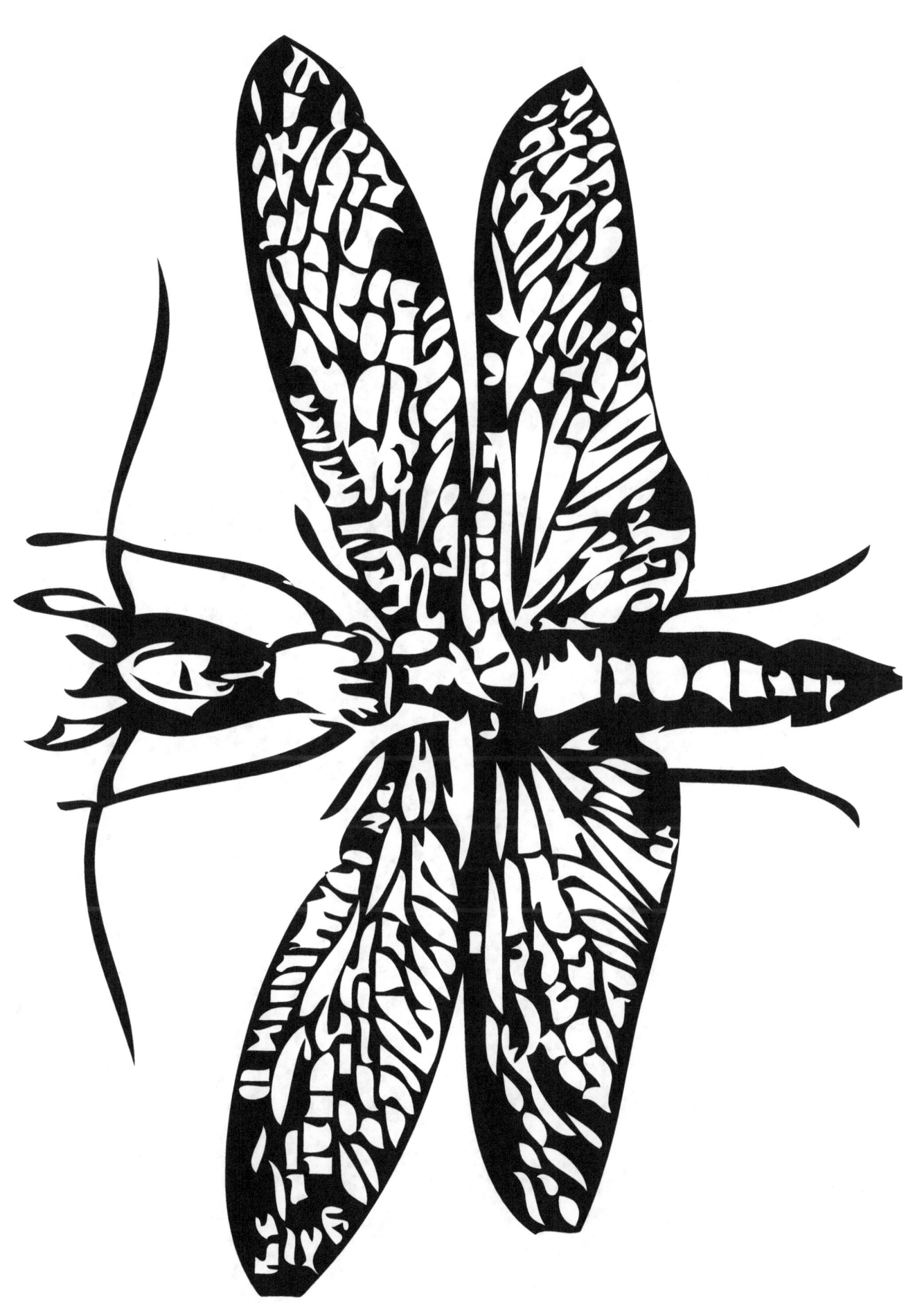

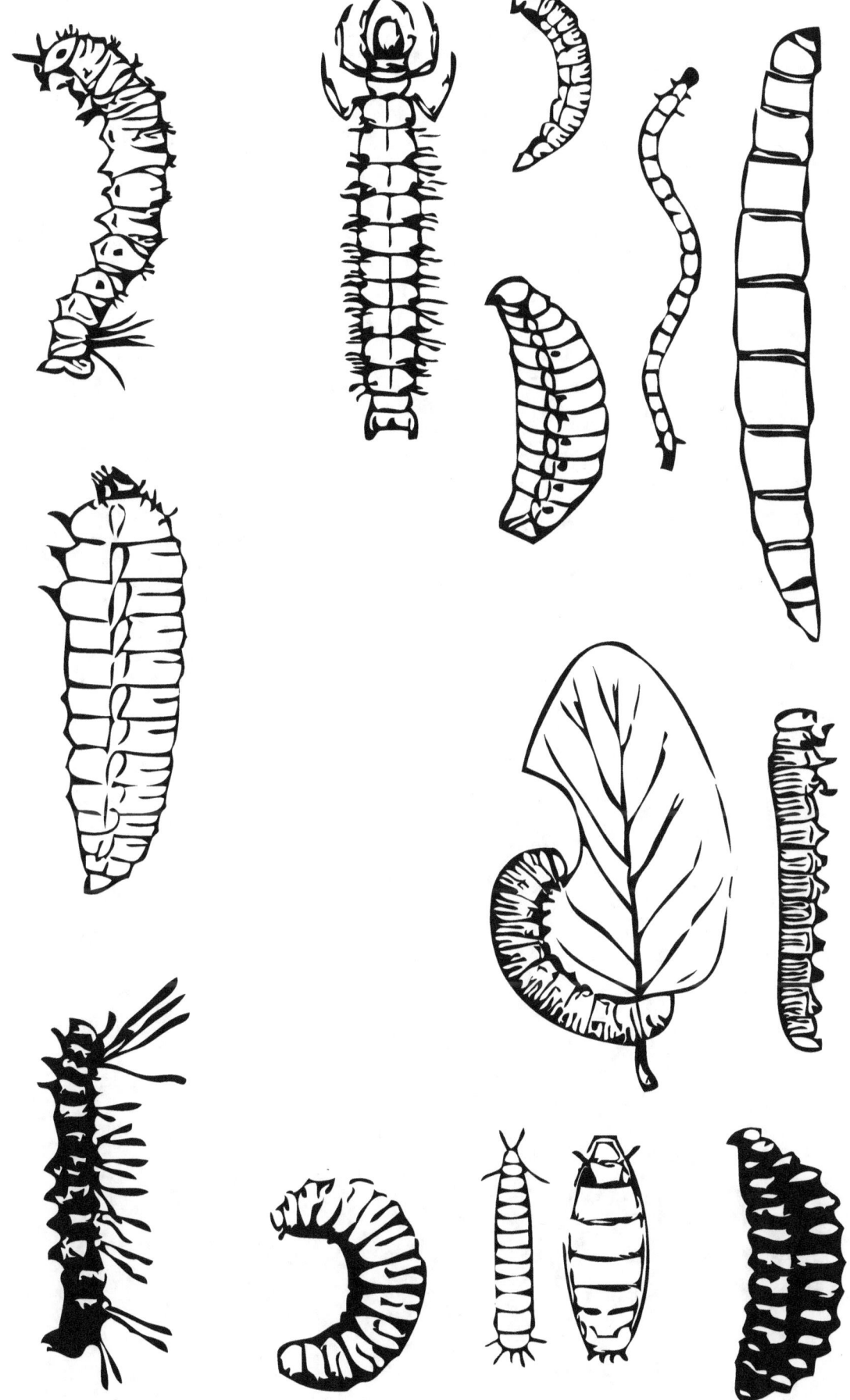

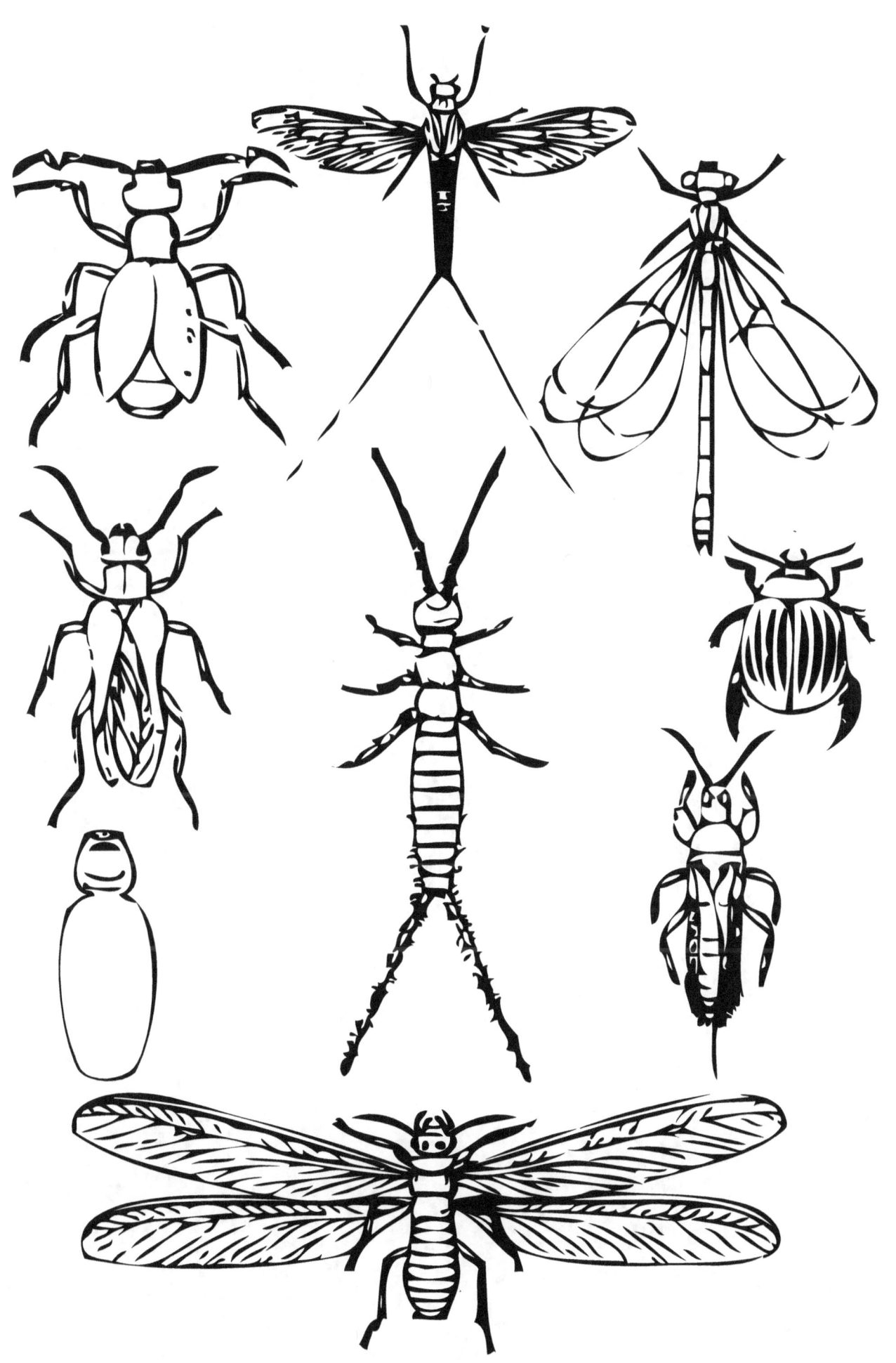

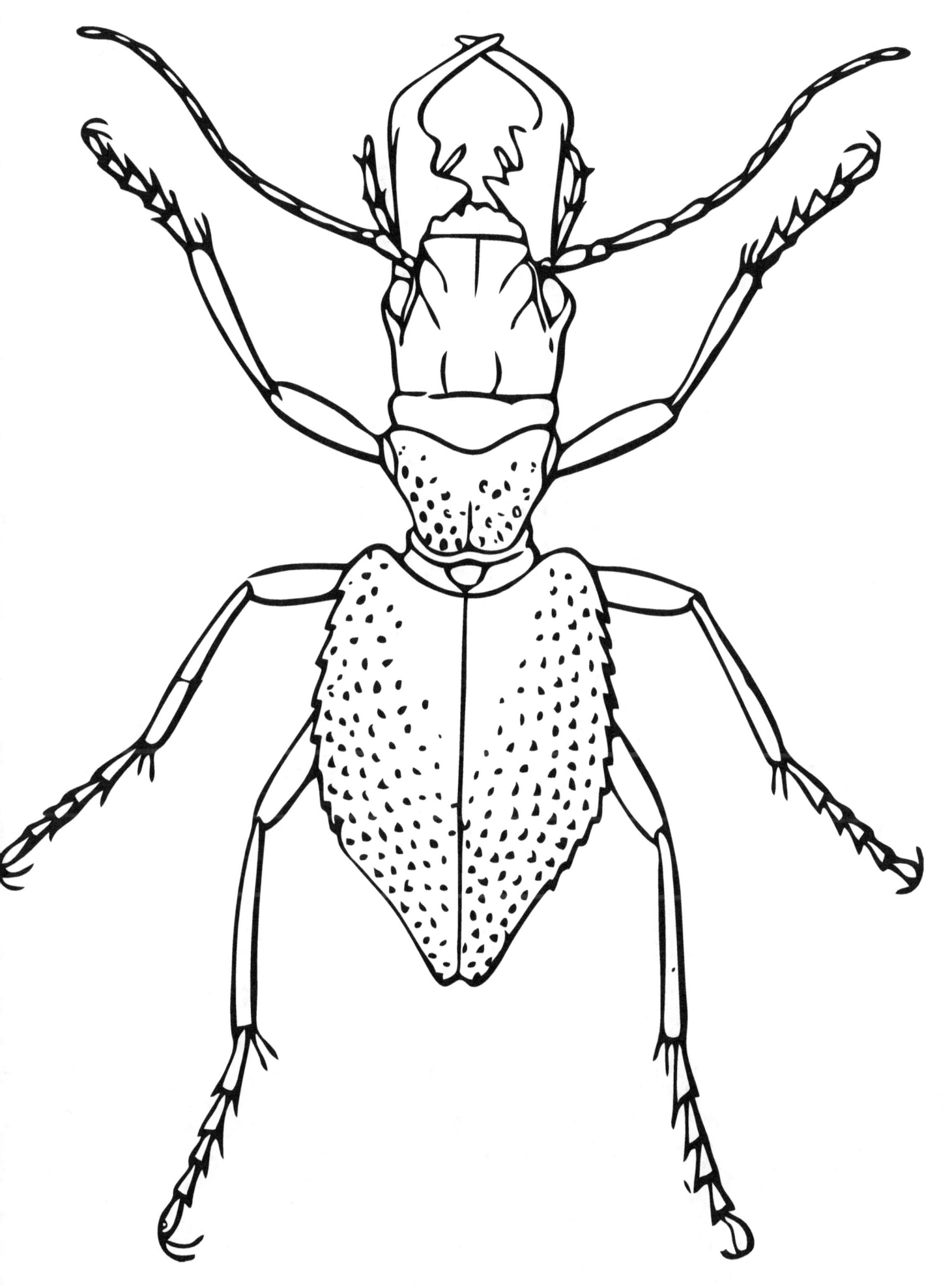

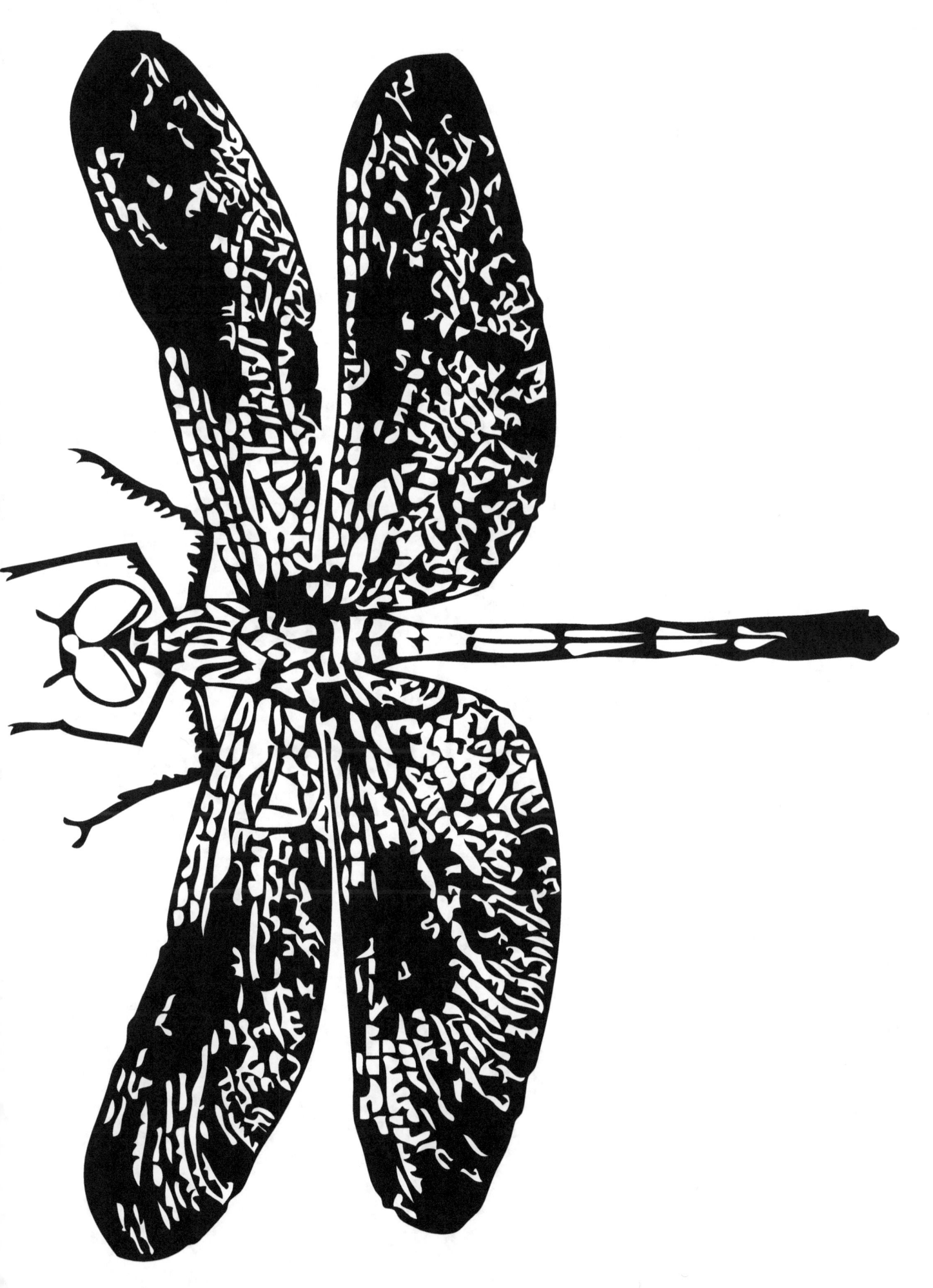

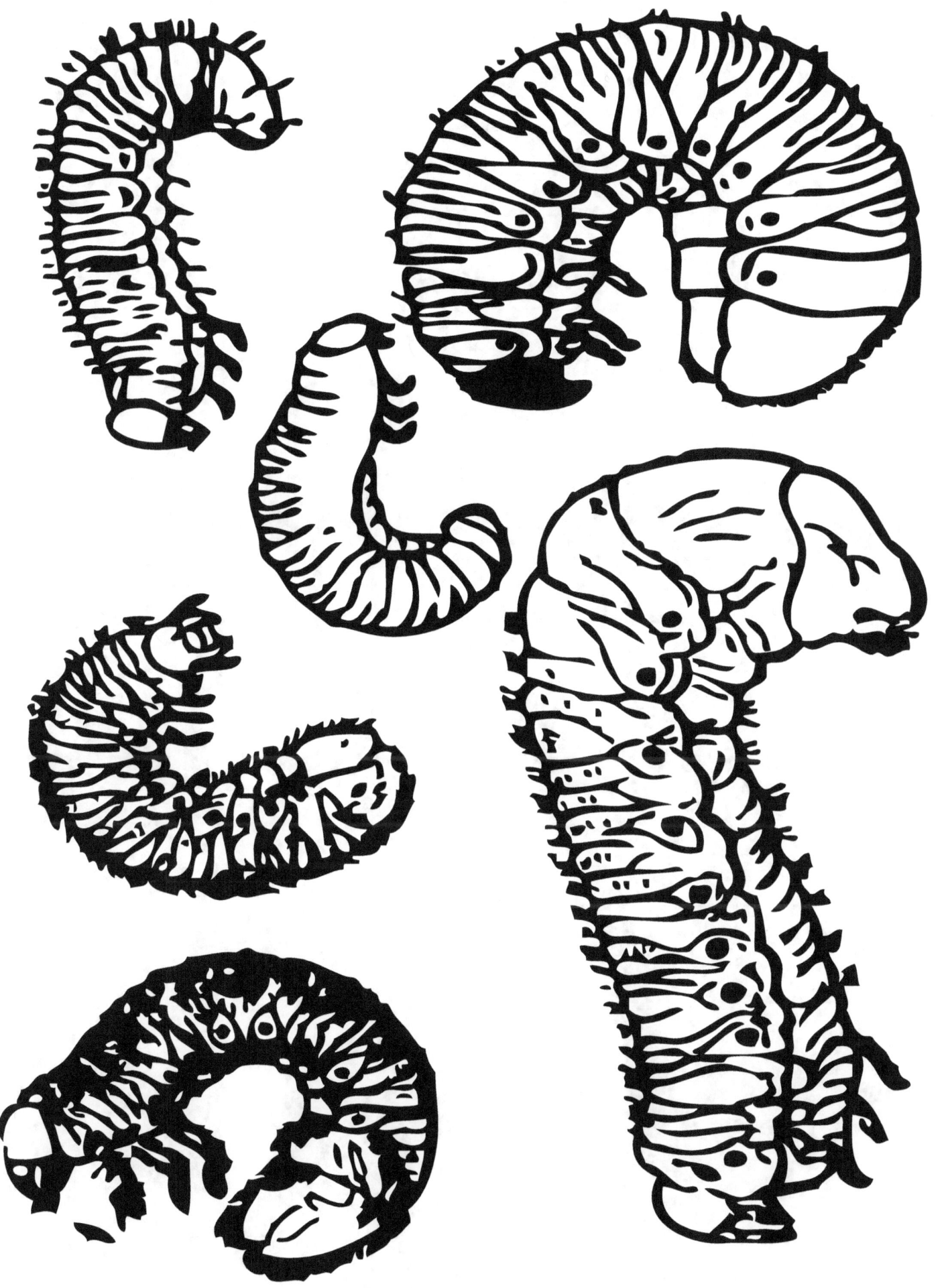

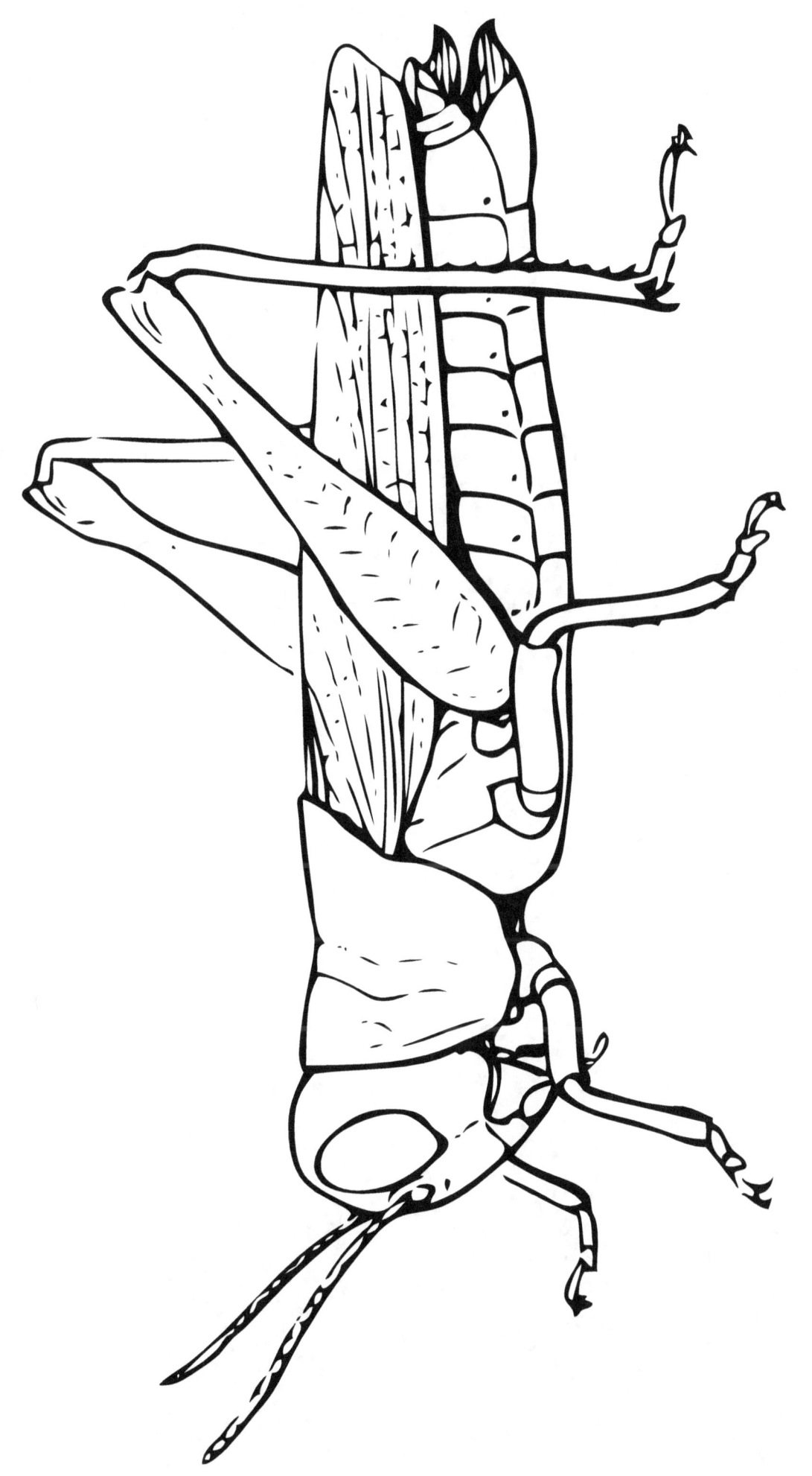

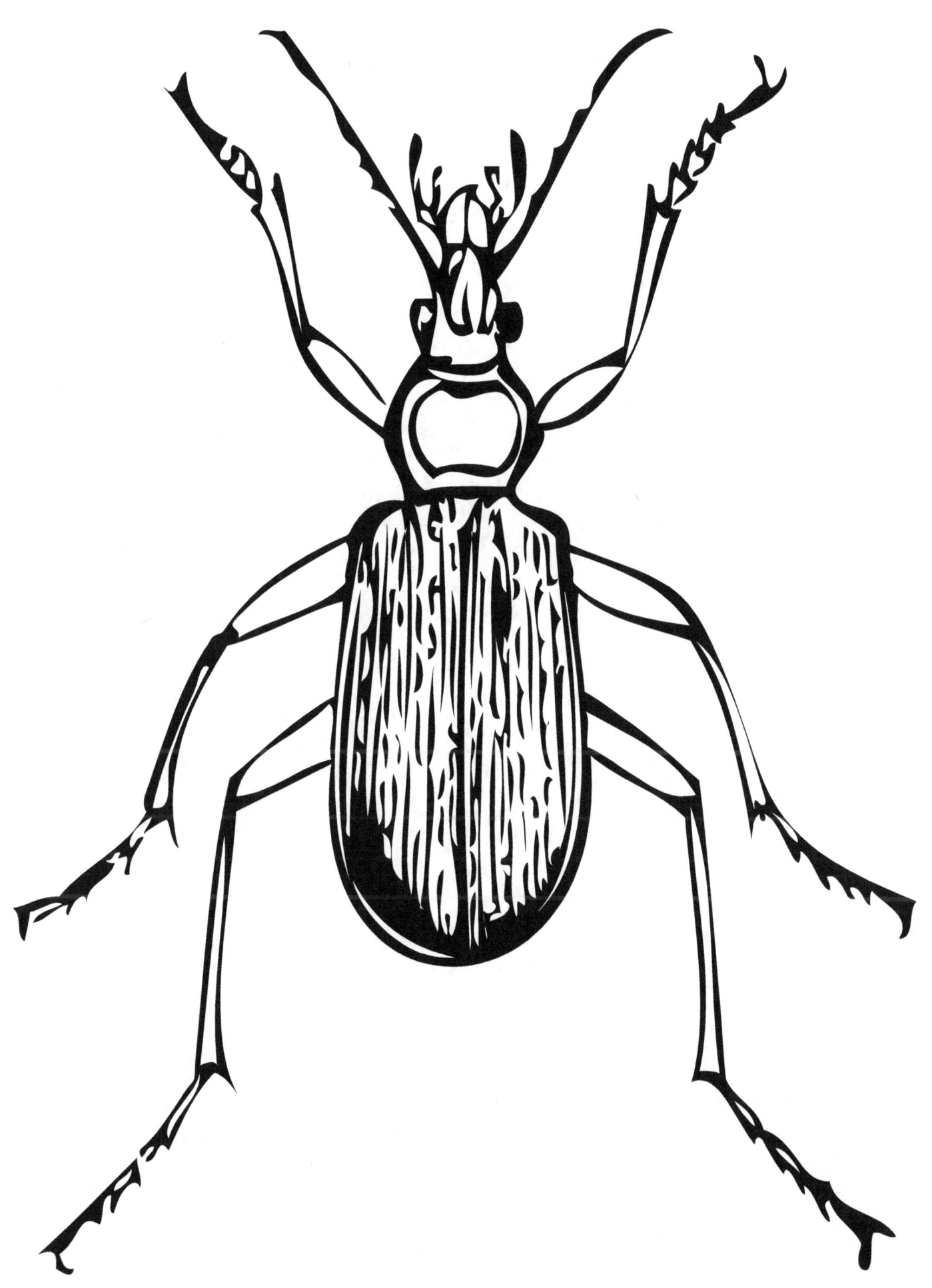

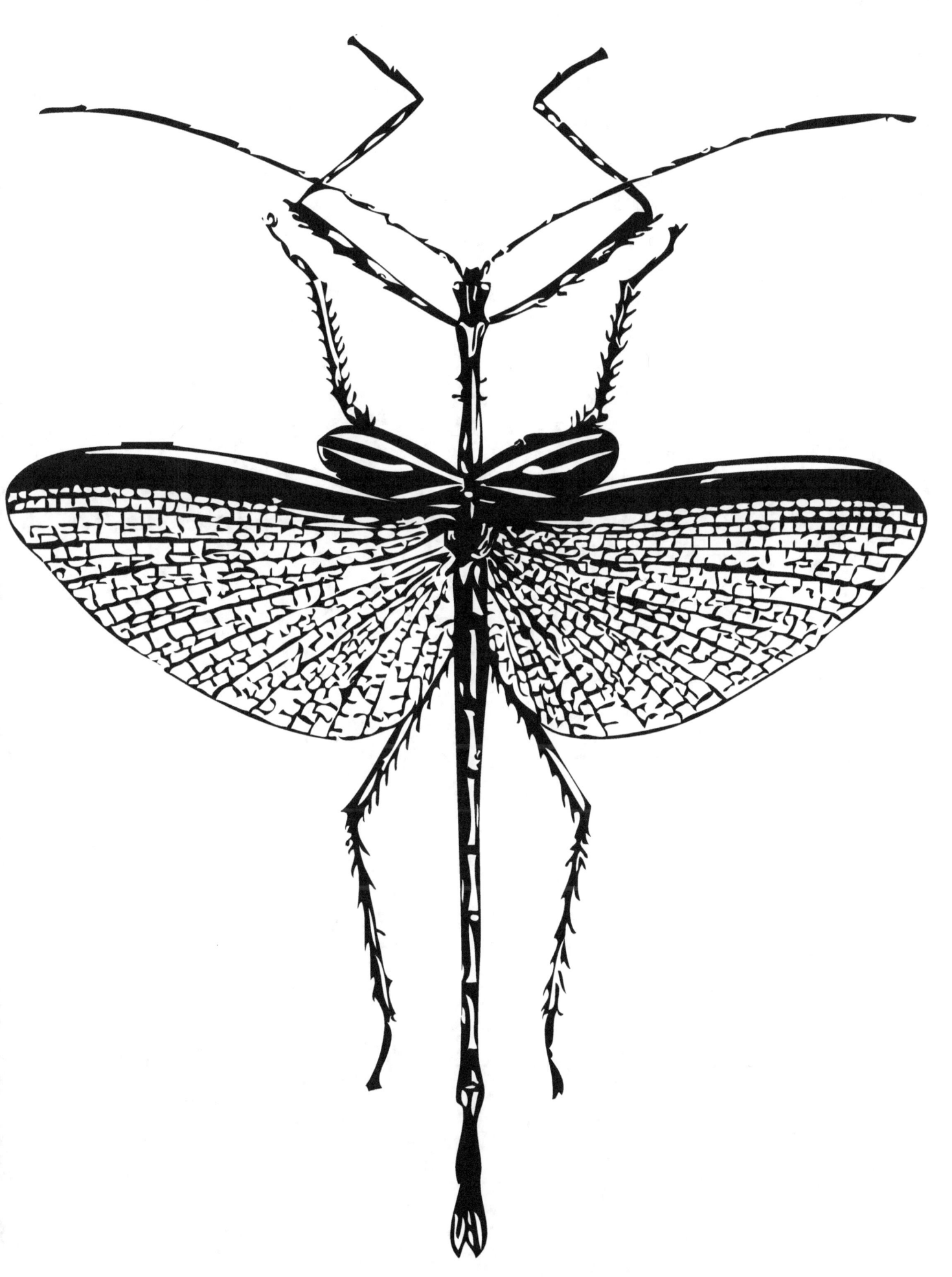

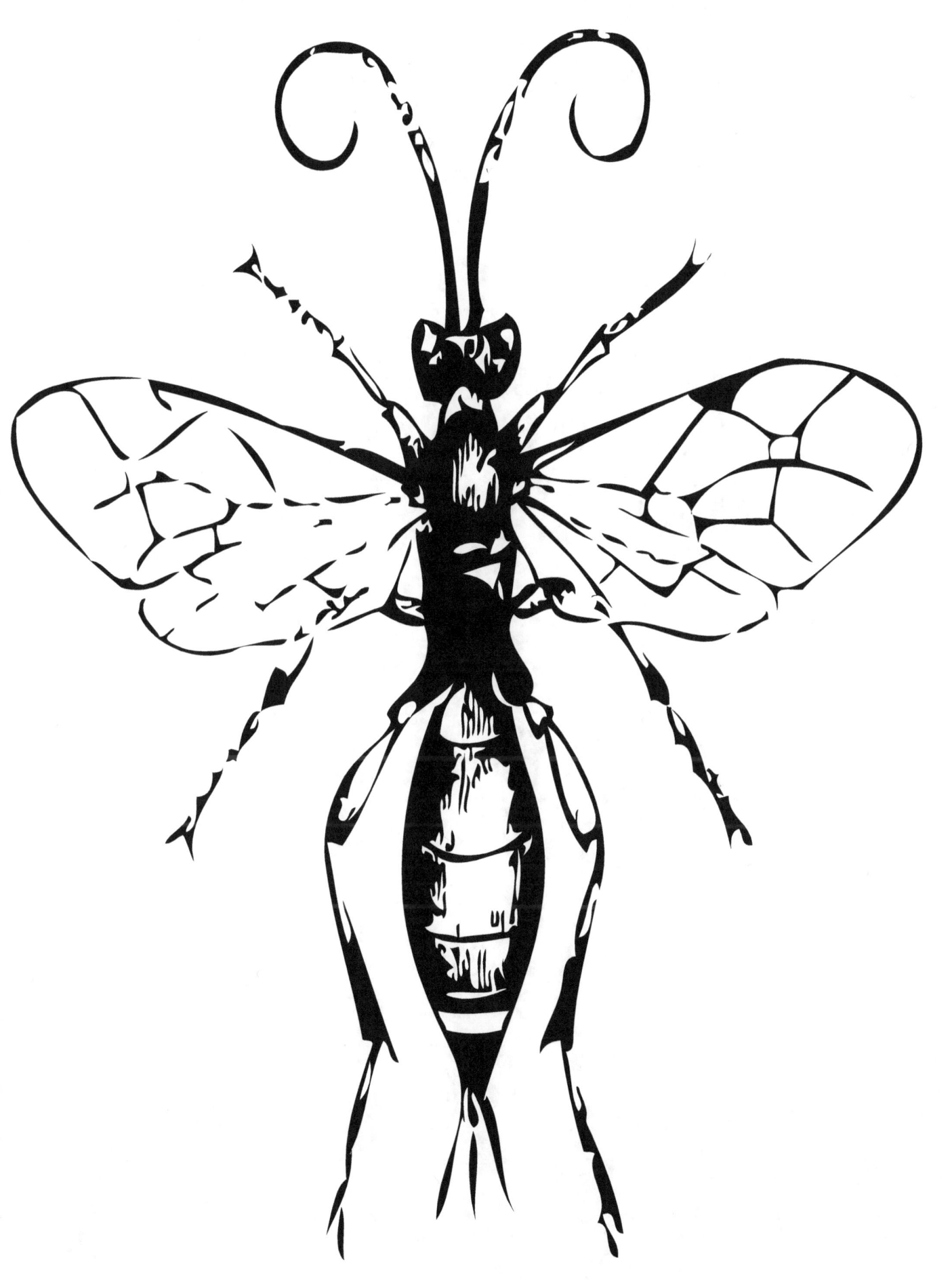

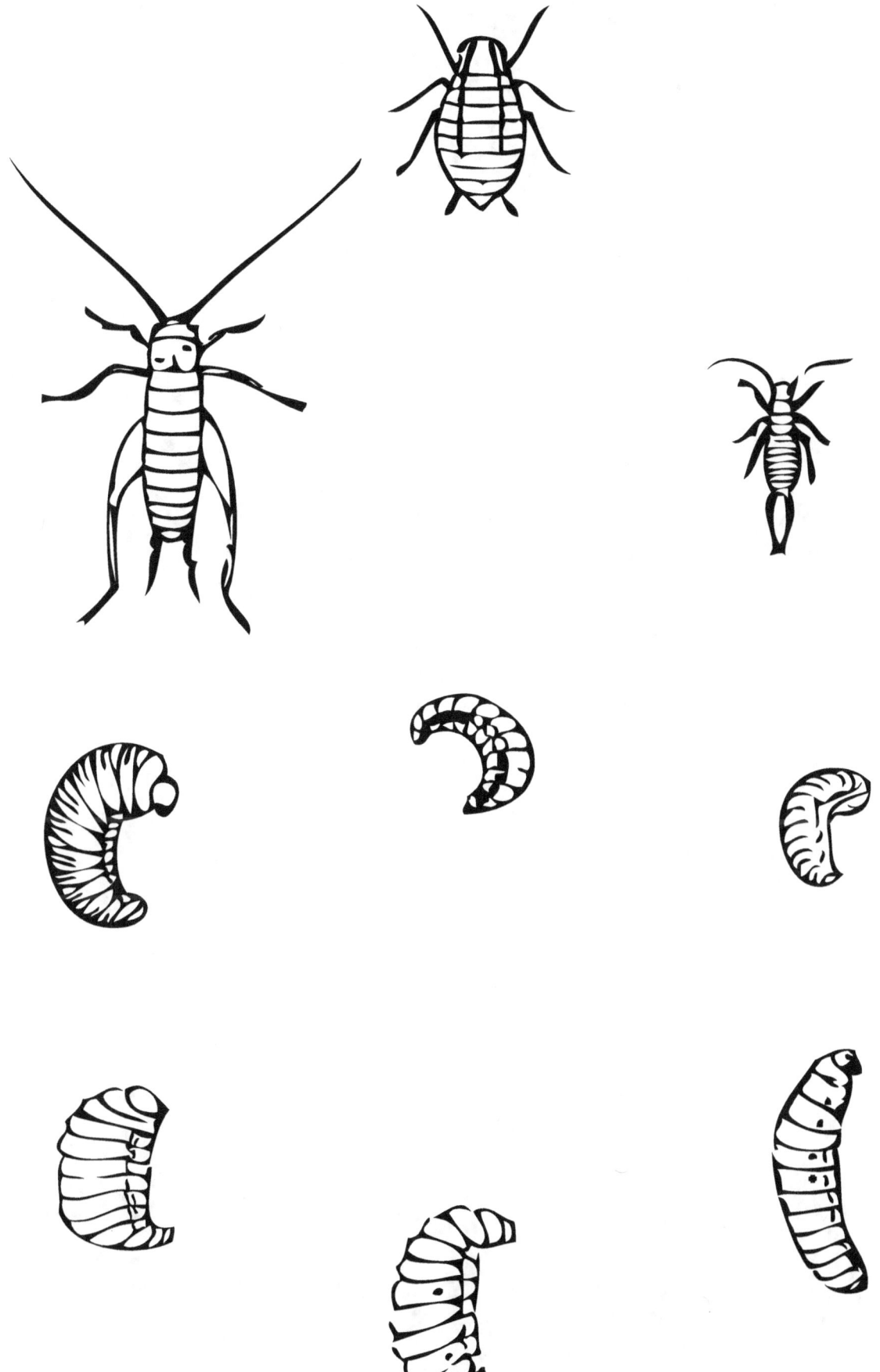

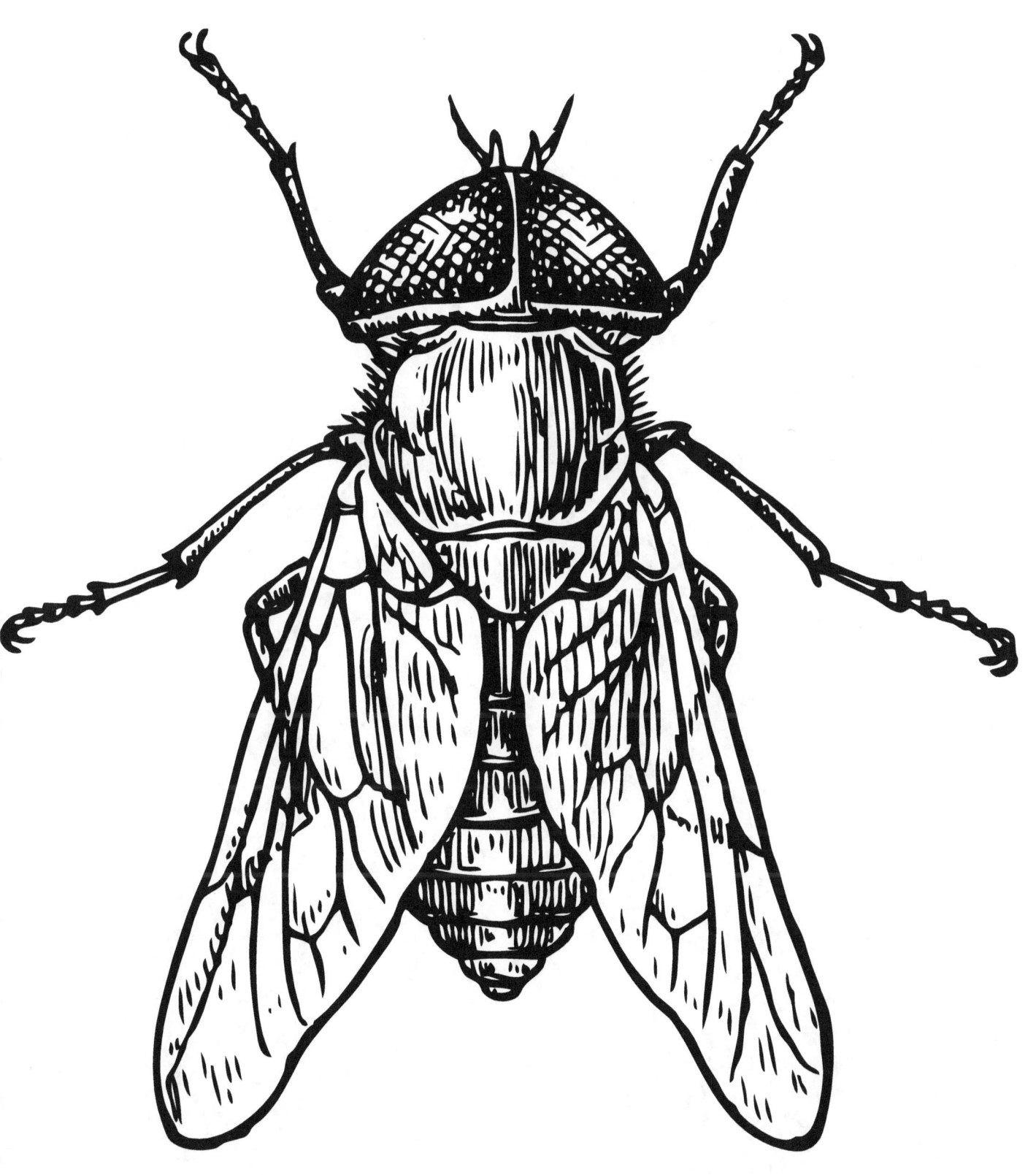

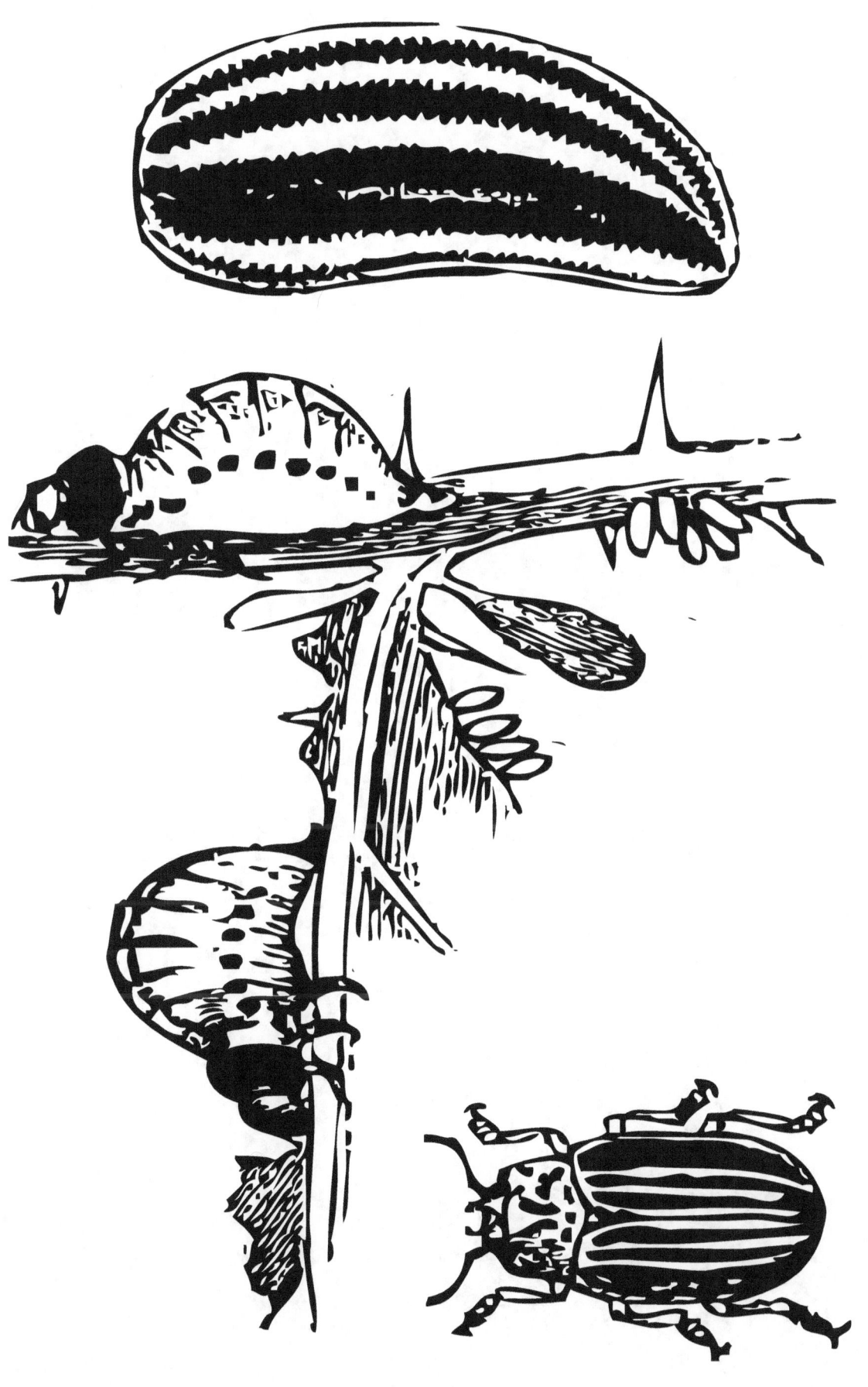

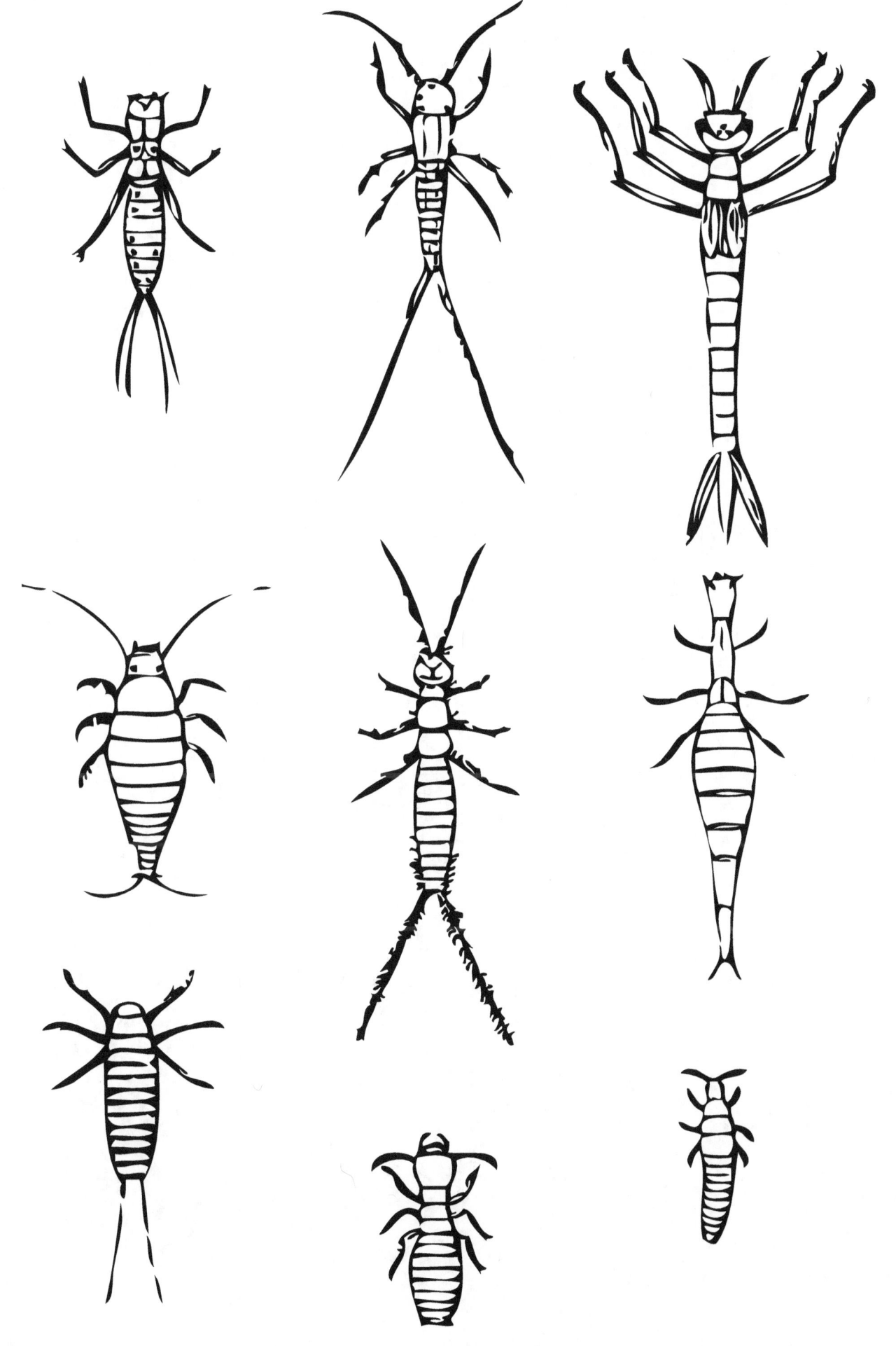

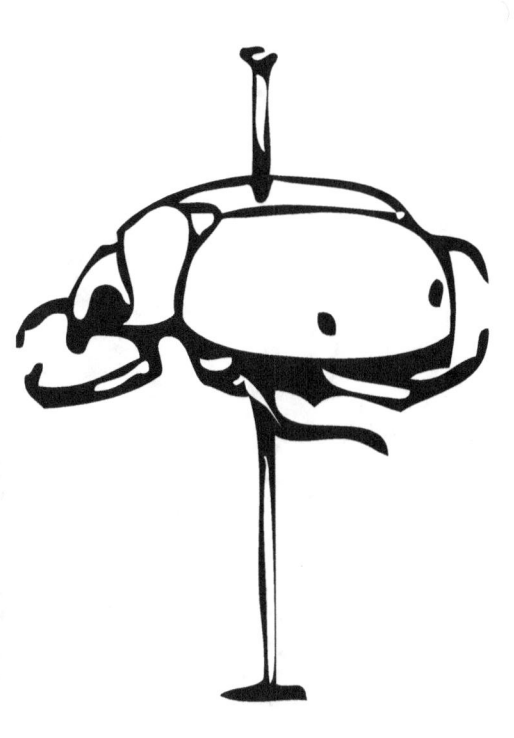
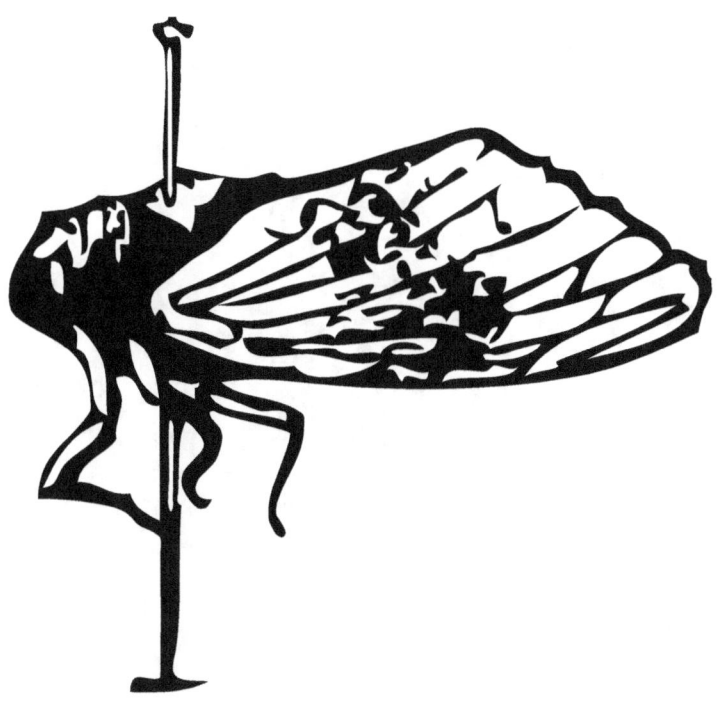

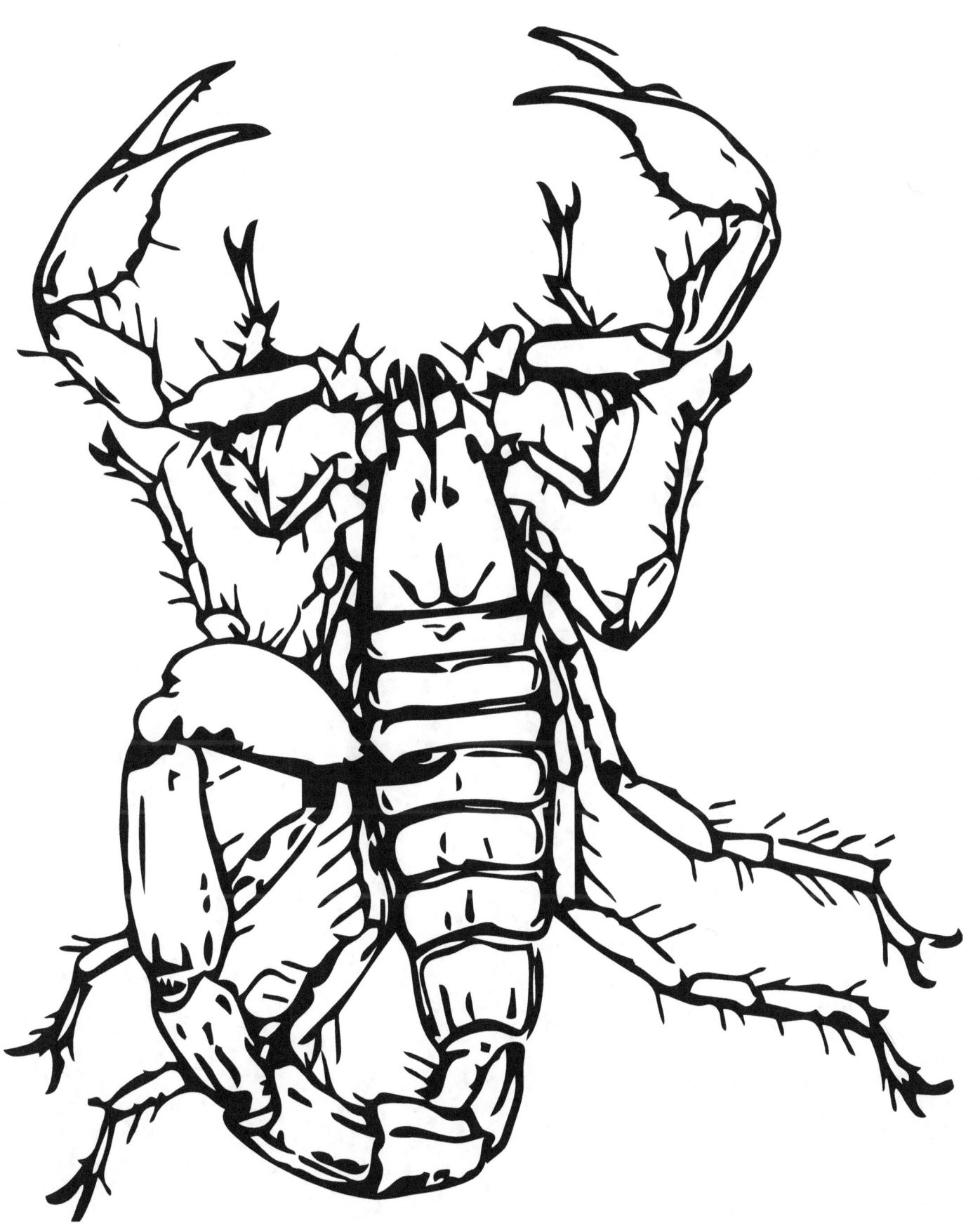

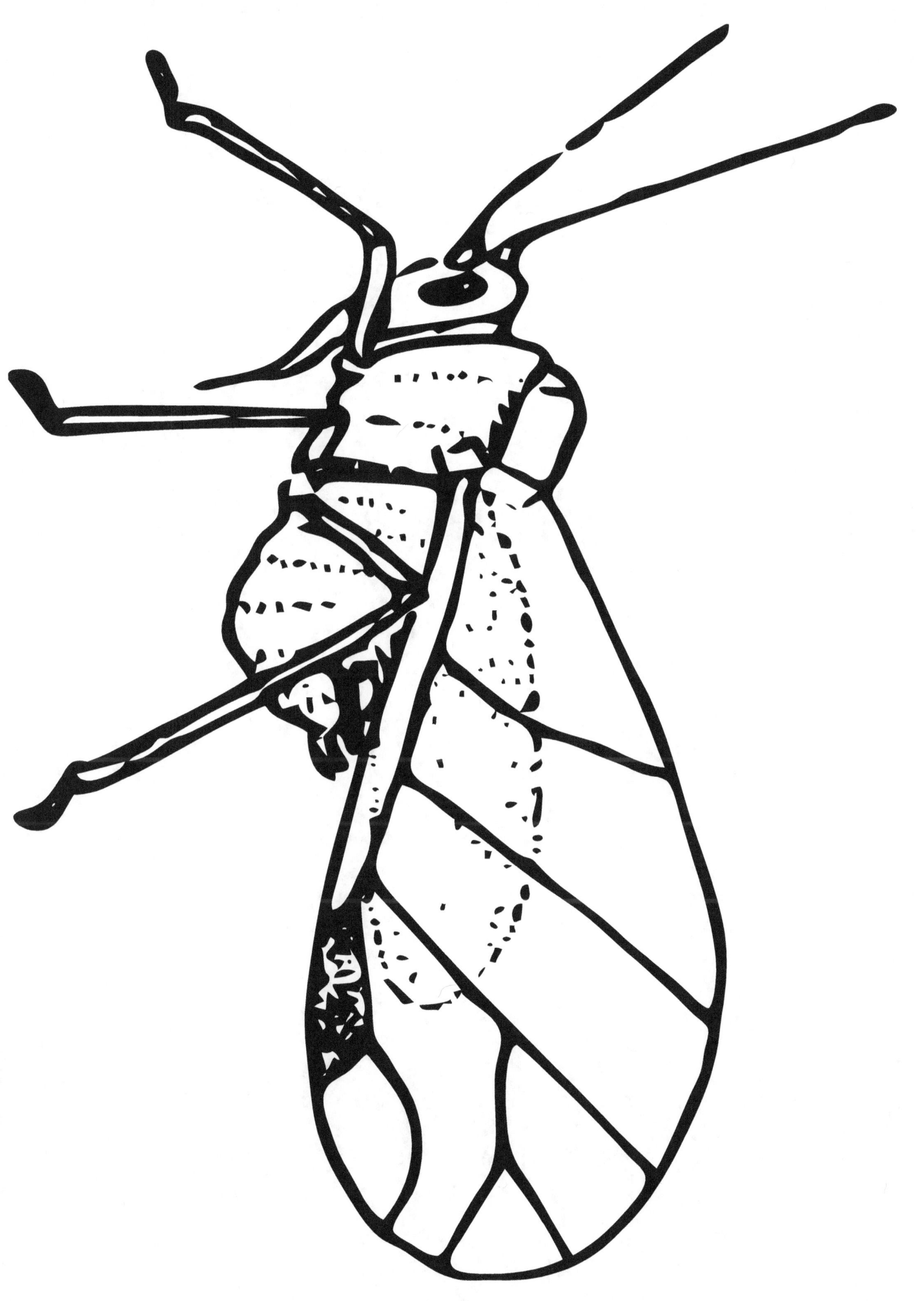

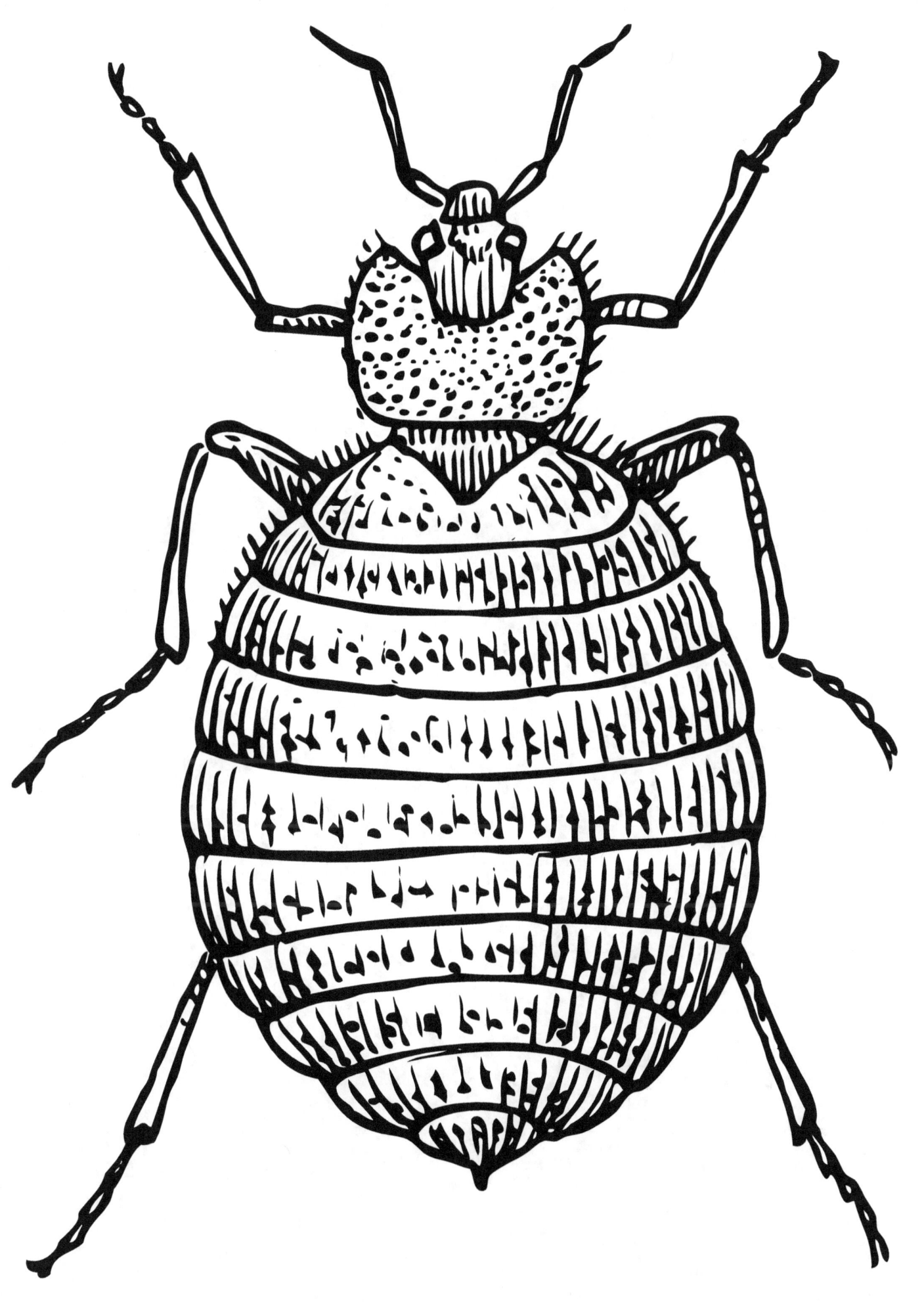

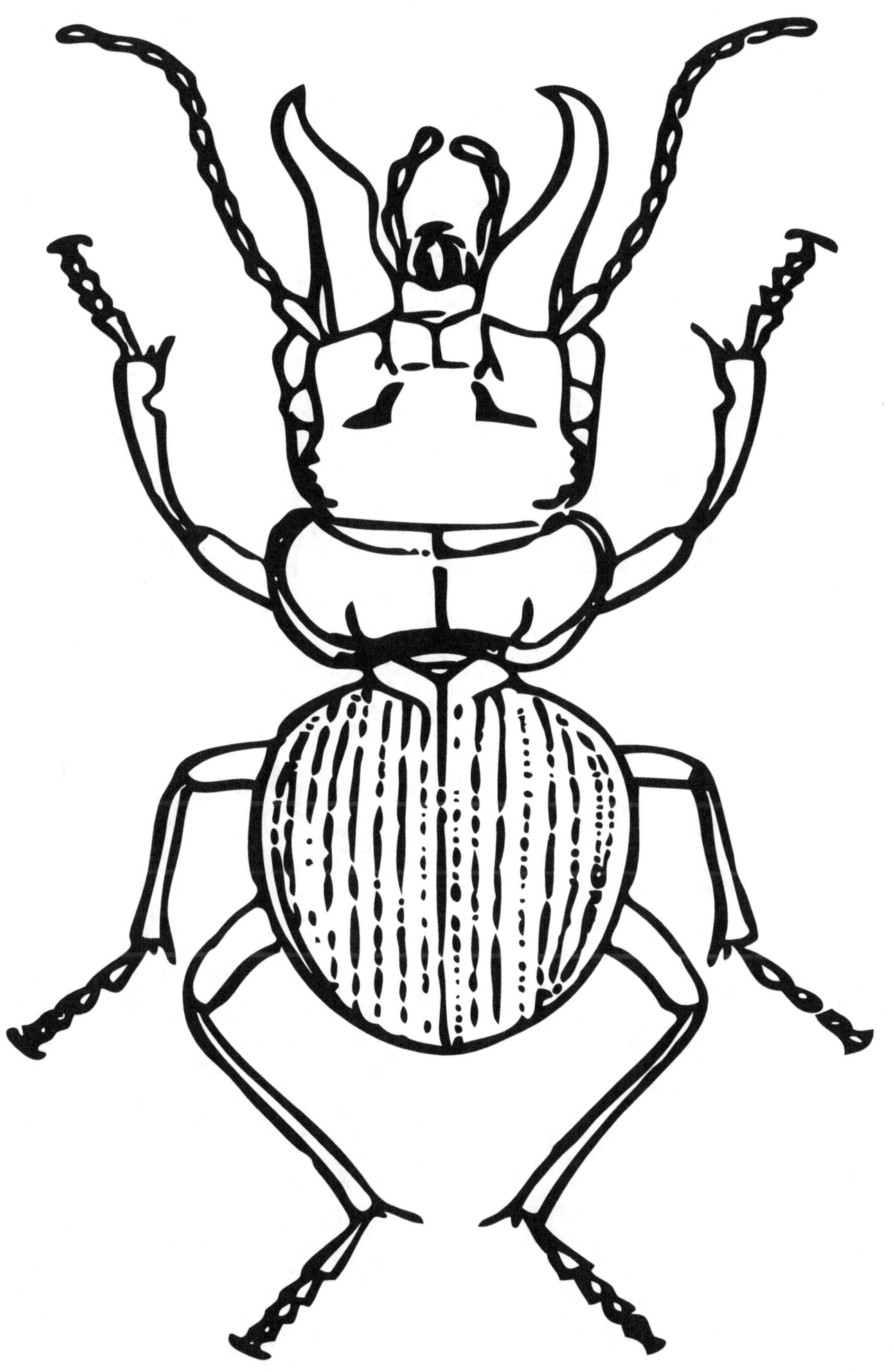

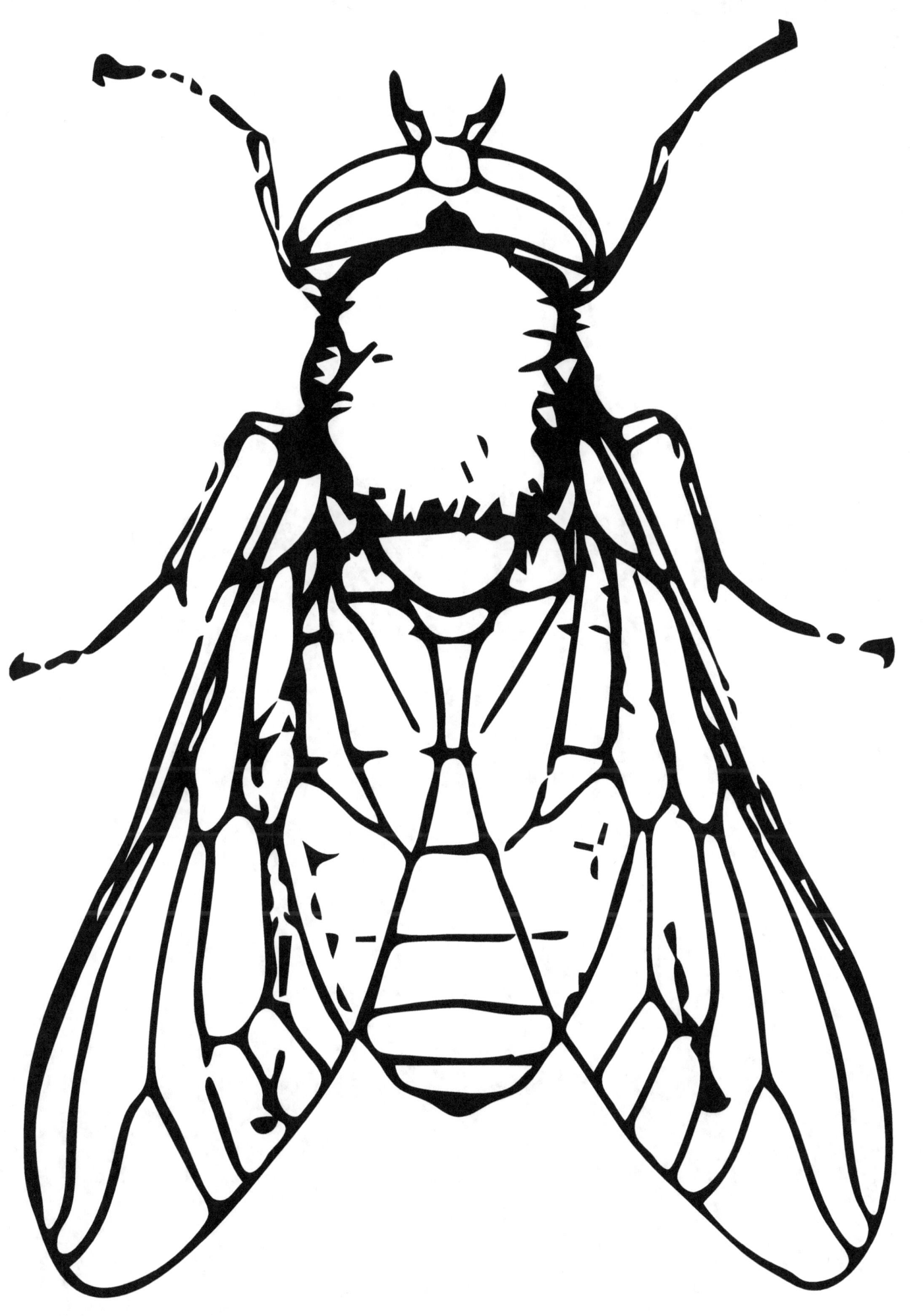

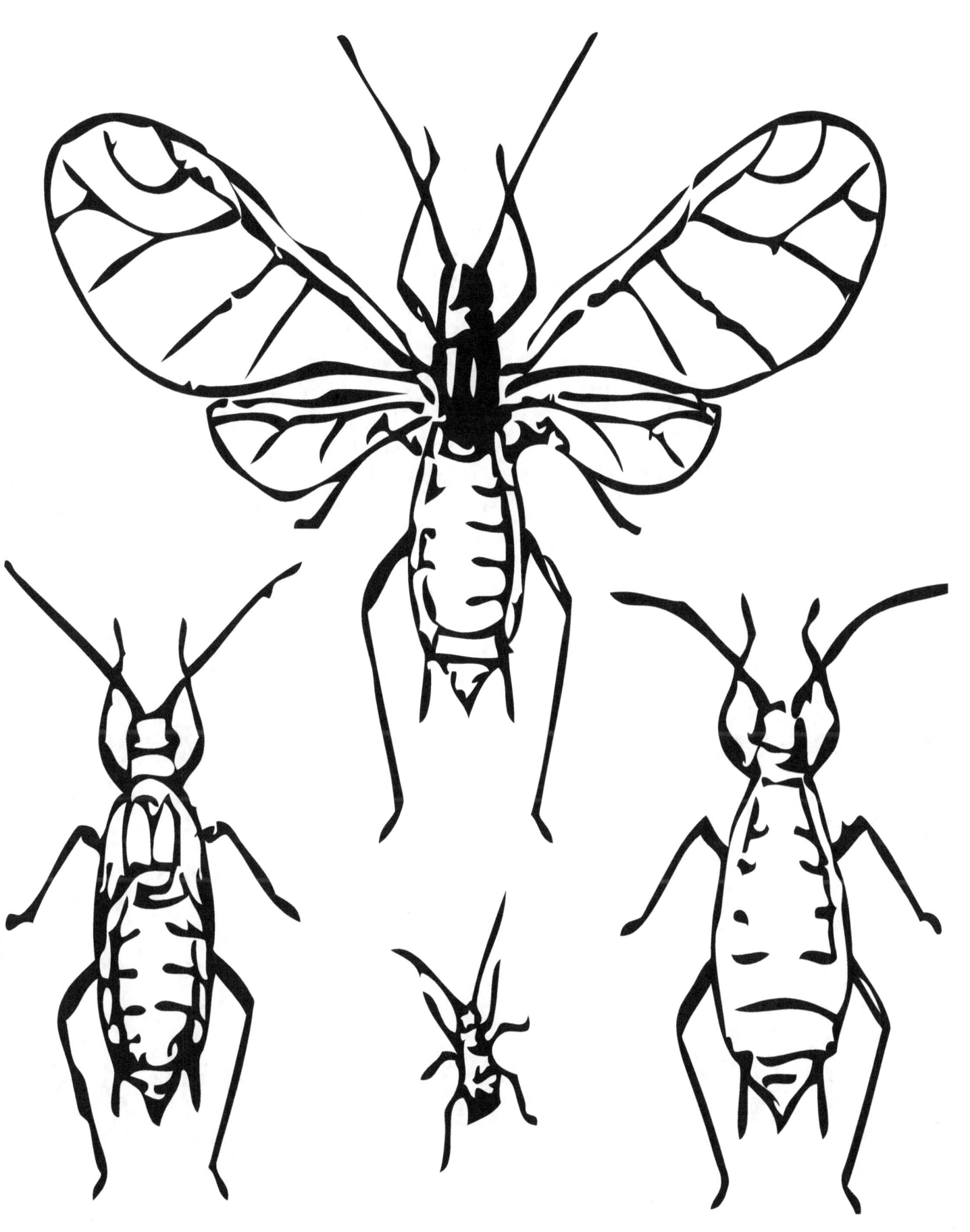

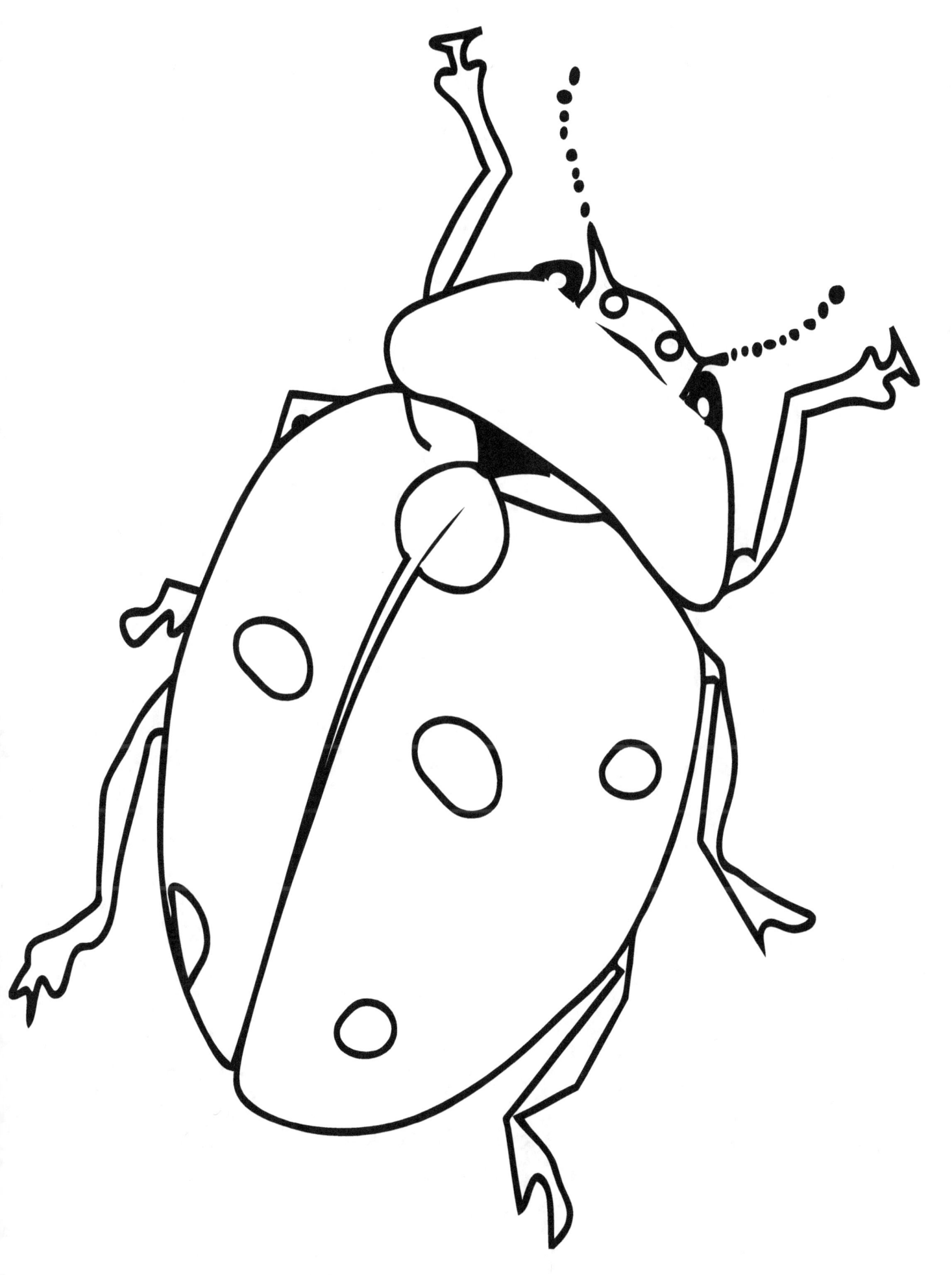

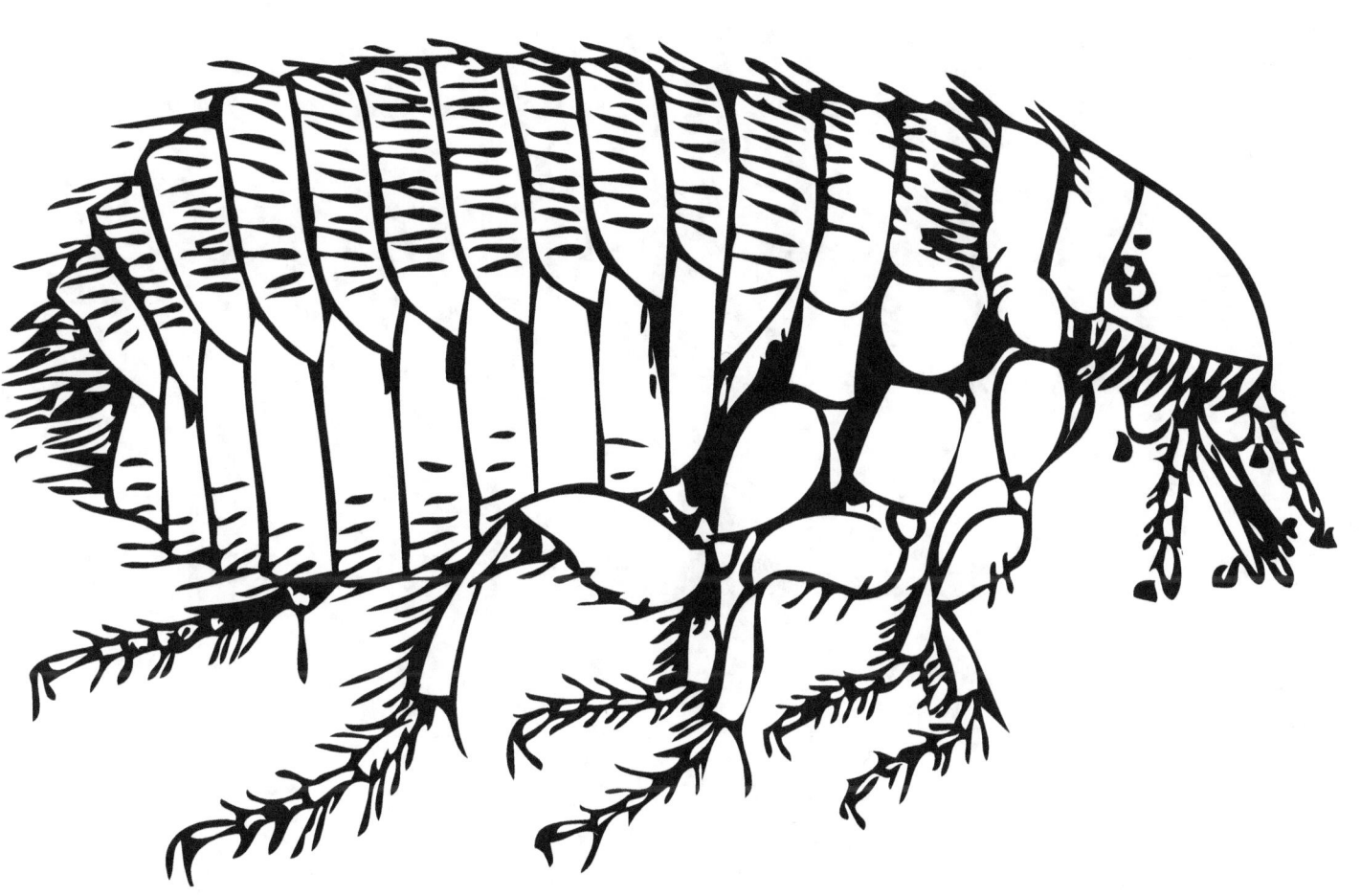

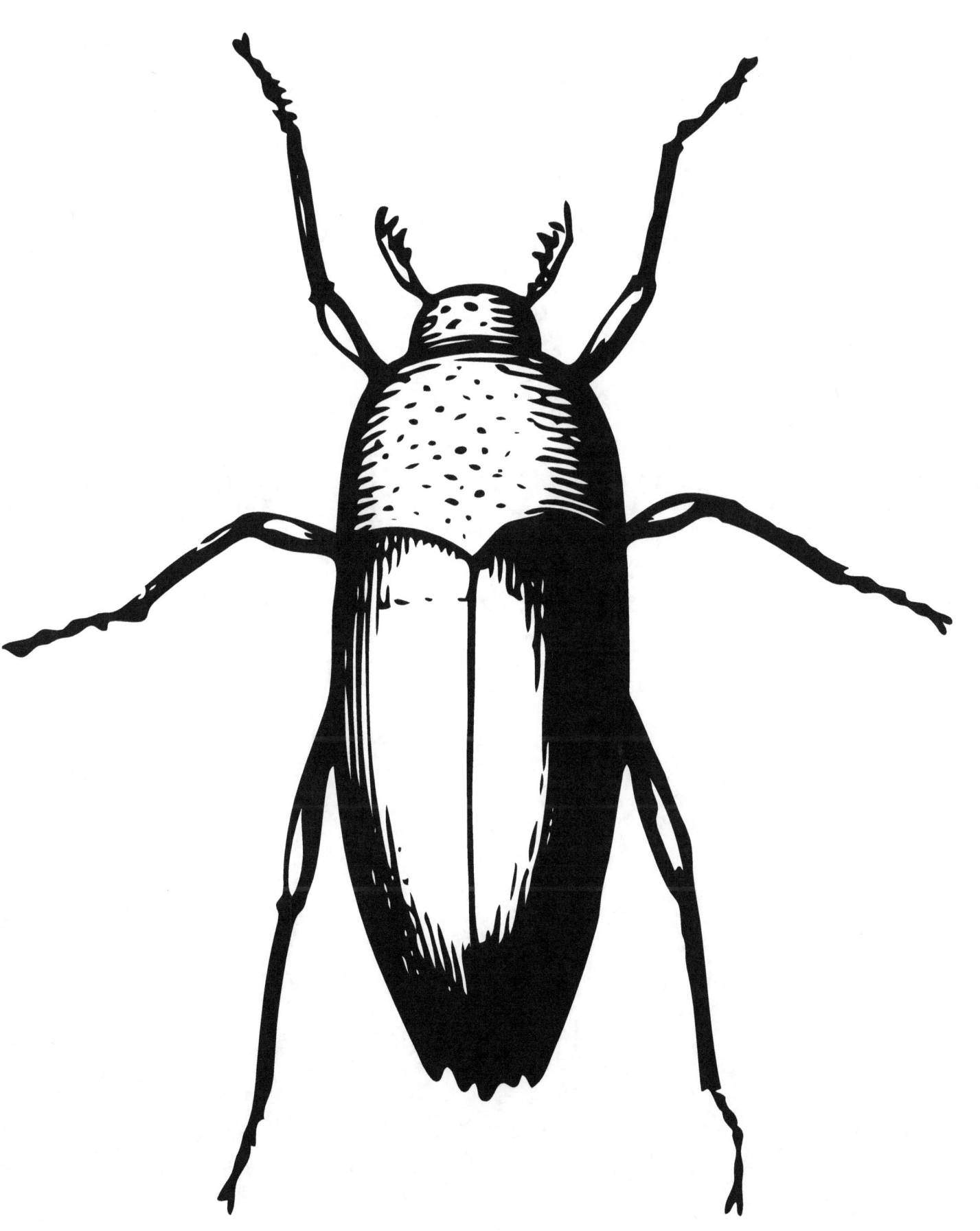

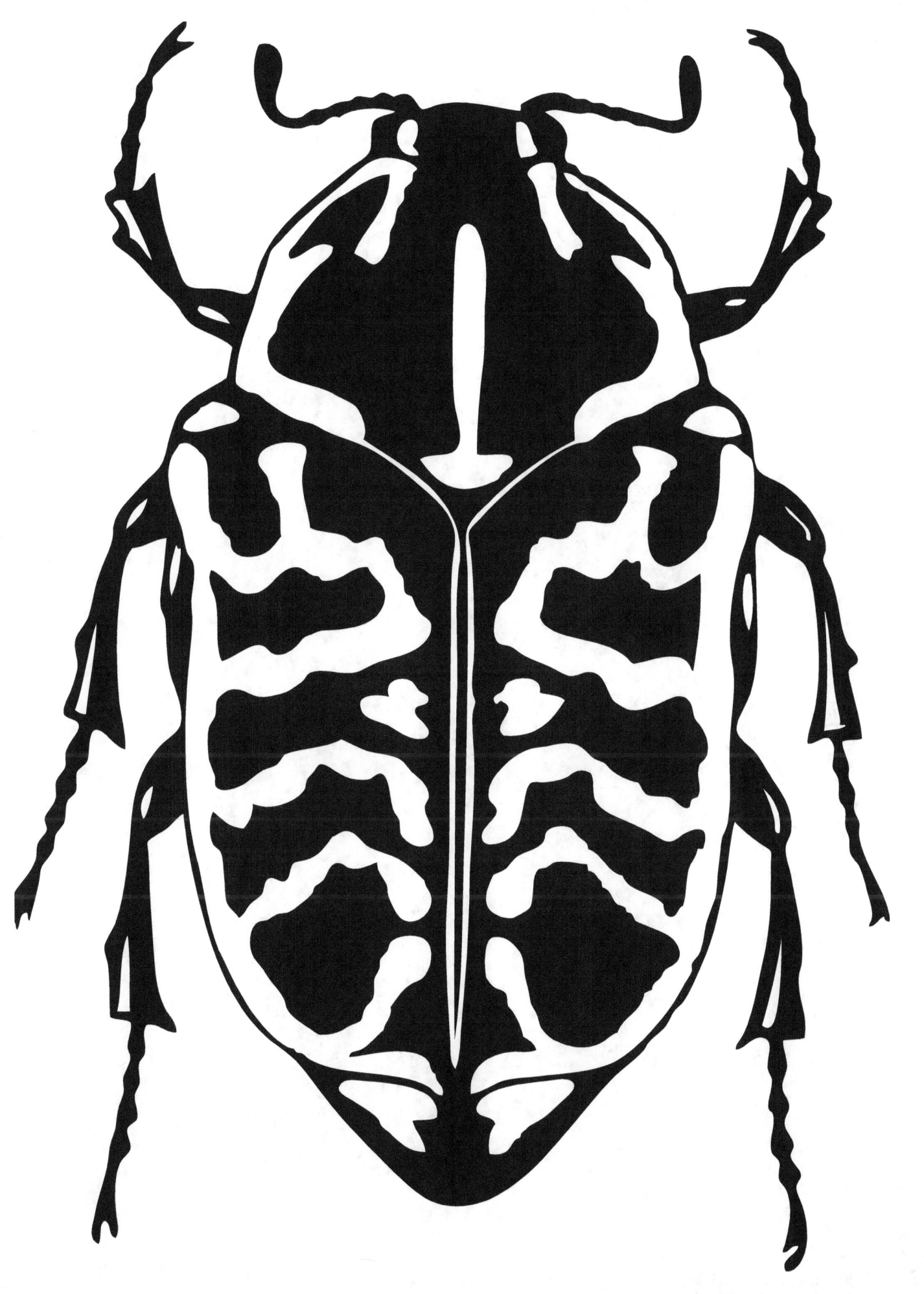

www.ingramcontent.com/pod-product-compliance
Lightning Source LLC
Chambersburg PA
CBHW081228280526
45787CB00006B/2565